▪ PEOPLES OF AFRICA ▪

PEOPLES OF NORTH AFRICA

THE DIAGRAM GROUP

Facts On File, Inc.

Peoples of Africa: Peoples of North Africa

Copyright © 1997 by The Diagram Group

Diagram Visual Information Ltd

Editorial director:	Bridget Giles
Contributors:	Trevor Day, Theodore Rowland Entwistle, David Lambert, Keith Lye, Oliver Marshall, Christopher Priest
Editors:	Margaret Doyle, Moira Johnston, Ian Wood
Indexer:	David Harding
Art director/designer:	Philip Patenall
Artists:	Chris Allcott, Darren Bennett, Bob Garwood, Elsa Godfrey, Brian Hewson, Kyri Kyriacou, Janos Marffy, Kathy McDougall Patrick Mulrey, Rob Shone, Graham Rosewarne, Peter Ross
Production director:	Richard Hummerstone
Production:	Mark Carry, Lee Lawrence, Ollie Madden, Philip Richardson, Dave Wilson
Research director:	Matt Smout
Researchers:	Pamela Kea, Chris Owens, Catherine Michard, Neil McKenna

With the assistance of:

Dr. Elizabeth Dunstan, International African Institute, School of Oriental and African Studies, University of London

David Hall, African studies bibliographer at the School of Oriental and African Studies, University of London

Horniman Museum, London

Museum of Mankind library, British Museum

Survival International

WWF-UK

Facts On File, Inc.
11 Penn Plaza
New York NY 10001

Library of Congress Cataloging-in-Publication Data

Peoples of North Africa / the Diagram Group.
     p.   cm. – (Peoples of Africa)
  Includes index.
  ISBN 0-8160-3483-4 (alk. paper)
  1. Ethnology–Africa, North. 2. Africa, North–Social life and customs. I. Diagram Group. II. Series: Peoples of Africa (New York, N.Y.)
DT192.P466   1997
961'.004–DC20   96-41273

Facts On File books are available at special discounts when purchased in bulk quantities for businesses, associations, institutions, or sales promotions. Please call our Special Sales Department in New York at 212/967-8800 or 800/322-8755.

You can find Facts On File on the World Wide Web at http://www.factsonfile.com

Cover design by Molly Heron

Printed in the United States of America

RRD DIAG 10 9 8 7 6 5 4 3

This book is printed on acid-free paper

Contents

Foreword

Peoples of North Africa, the first volume in the Facts On File *Peoples of Africa* series, focuses on the historical and cultural richness of the north of the continent. This area covers the nations of Algeria, Egypt, Libya, Morocco, Sudan, and Tunisia, and the disputed territory of Western Sahara, which is occupied by Morocco.

Inside this volume the reader will find:

- **The region:** preliminary pages describing the region in depth – its land, climate, vegetation, and wildlife – and others providing a broad historical overview and a current political profile.

- **The people:** profiles of ten major ethnic groups within North Africa, describing the **history, language, ways of life, social structure,** and **culture and religion** of each group. Wherever possible, a map has been included for each ethnic group to show the general region that the group inhabits or is most concentrated in. The people profiles are arranged alphabetically. They are not encyclopedic; instead, they highlight particular aspects of a culture, focusing on fascinating details that will remain with the reader.

- **Special features:** tinted pages interspersed throughout the volume, each on a particular topical or cultural subject. Historical theme spreads, such as that on Ancient Egypt, demonstrate the lasting influence of communities and civilizations of the past. Still other features illustrate the great variety to be found in aspects of culture such as music, architecture, hairstyles, and foods.

- **Language appendix:** a diagrammatic outline of the African language families. It can be used to locate the languages of the peoples profiled and to see how they relate to other languages.

- **Glossary and index:** following the profiles, features, and appendix are a comprehensive glossary defining the unfamiliar terms used within the volume and a complete index to the volume. Words that appear in the glossary have been printed in roman in special features and *italics* elsewhere.

Taken as a whole, *Peoples of North Africa* is intended to project a living portrait of the region that, with the other volumes in the series, provides the reader with a memorable snapshot of Africa as a place of rich heritage, far-reaching influence, and ongoing cultural diversity.

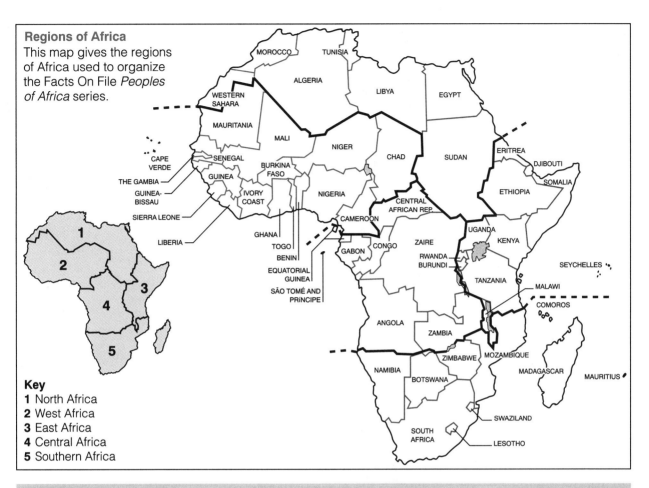

Regions of Africa

This map gives the regions of Africa used to organize the Facts On File *Peoples of Africa* series.

MOROCCO
TUNISIA
ALGERIA
LIBYA
EGYPT
WESTERN SAHARA
MAURITANIA
MALI
NIGER
CHAD
SUDAN
ERITREA
DJIBOUTI
SOMALIA
ETHIOPIA
CAPE VERDE
SENEGAL
THE GAMBIA
GUINEA-BISSAU
GUINEA
BURKINA FASO
SIERRA LEONE
IVORY COAST
NIGERIA
CENTRAL AFRICAN REP.
LIBERIA
GHANA
TOGO
BENIN
CAMEROON
EQUATORIAL GUINEA
SÃO TOMÉ AND PRÍNCIPE
GABON
CONGO
ZAIRE
UGANDA
KENYA
RWANDA
BURUNDI
TANZANIA
SEYCHELLES
MALAWI
COMOROS
ANGOLA
ZAMBIA
MOZAMBIQUE
MADAGASCAR
MAURITIUS
NAMIBIA
ZIMBABWE
BOTSWANA
SWAZILAND
SOUTH AFRICA
LESOTHO

Key
1 North Africa
2 West Africa
3 East Africa
4 Central Africa
5 Southern Africa

A word about ethnic groups

The series *Peoples of Africa* focuses on ethnic groups or peoples, useful but difficult-to-define terms. In the past, the word "tribe" was used to describe ethnic groupings, but this is today considered an offensive and arbitrary label. It is incorrect to refer to a group of people who may number in the hundreds of thousands and who have a long history of nation building as a tribe. "Tribe" is now generally used only to describe a basic political unit that exists within some larger ethnic groups, not to describe the group itself. So what is an ethnic group? An ethnic group is distinct from race or nationality; the former is rarely used today because it requires broad and inaccurate generalizations; and the latter describes only the national boundaries within which a person is born or lives. Both categories are fraught with difficulty. For the purposes of this series, the term "ethnic group" is used to describe people who have a common language, history, religion, and cultural and artistic heritage; they may also have a common way of life and often live within the same geographical area.

There are probably more than a thousand ethnic groups in all of Africa. Many are related to one another, often in complex ways. Groups have subgroups and even sub-subgroups. Intermarriage, colonialism, conquest, and migration through the ages have led to many combinations and to an intermixing of influences. In our series we have chosen to focus on only a fraction of Africa's many ethnic groups. A number of factors – including population figures, available information, and recognition outside Africa – were used in making the selection. To a certain extent, however, it was an arbitrary choice, but one that we hope offers a vibrant picture of the people of this continent.

North Africa today

North Africa is one of the continent's more prosperous regions. This is largely because of the huge reserves of oil and natural gas beneath the deserts, especially in Algeria and Libya. Another reason is that most North African countries have more stable economies than other African countries. With few exceptions, the sub-Saharan countries are economically dependent on agriculture and the export of raw

materials – agricultural and mineral – the prices of which fluctuate on the world market. North Africa faces its own problems, however. The economy of Sudan, the region's poorest country, has been drained by a long civil war between the Muslim north and the mainly non-Muslim south. In Algeria and Egypt, many people resent Western influences and support radical Islamic fundamentalist movements, which they see as the best means of preserving their culture. A hangover from colonial days is the unresolved issue of Western Sahara. This phosphate-rich, desert territory has been occupied by Morocco – for a while jointly with Mauritania – since Spain withdrew in 1975. Support for Saharan nationalists from other African countries has isolated Morocco, which left the Organization of African Unity (OAU) in protest.

Algiers · Annaba · Tunis
Mediterranean Sea
Oran · Constantine
TUNISIA
Tangier · Kenitra · Fez · Oujda
Rabat · Casablanca
Tripoli
Atlas Mountains
Marrakech
MOROCCO
Atlantic Ocean
ALGERIA
LIBYA
El Aaiún
SAHARA DESERT
WESTERN SAHARA

—— Country border
〜〜 River
Algiers Capital city

Major city populations
- ◼ Over 1,000,000
- ● 500,000 to 1,000,000
- ▪ 300,000 to 500,000
- · Under 300,000

| 0 | 200 | 400 | 600 | 800 km |
| 0 | 100 | 200 | 300 | 400 | 500 mi |

Country	Population (1994: 000s)	Area (sq. mi)	Per capita GNP (1994: US$)
Algeria	27,325	919,355	1650
Egypt	61,636	386,095	720
Libya	5,225	679,180	8,355 (1992)
Morocco	26,488	177,115	1,140
Sudan	27,361	967,245	675 (1992)
Tunisia	8,733	63,360	1,790
Western Sahara	272	97,345	NA

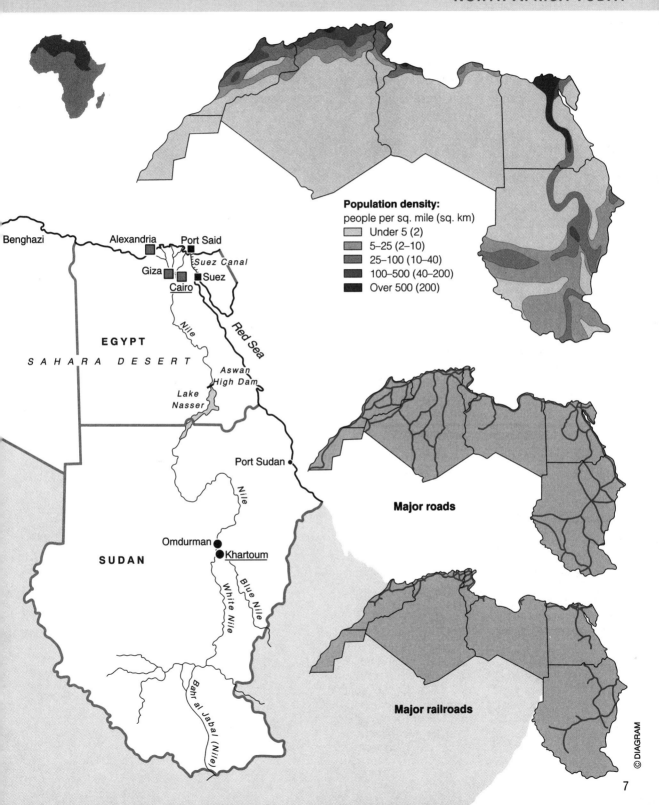

Population density:
people per sq. mile (sq. km)
- Under 5 (2)
- 5–25 (2–10)
- 25–100 (10–40)
- 100–500 (40–200)
- Over 500 (200)

Benghazi

Alexandria

Port Said

Suez Canal

Giza

Suez

Cairo

Nile

Red Sea

EGYPT

S A H A R A   D E S E R T

Aswan
High Dam

*Lake
Nasser*

Port Sudan

Nile

SUDAN

Omdurman

Khartoum

White Nile

Blue Nile

*Bahr al Jabal
(Nile)*

Major roads

Major railroads

© DIAGRAM

7

Land

North Africa is a largely desert region stretching from the Atlantic Ocean in the west to the Red Sea in the east. It is bordered by the Mediterranean Sea in the north and to the south by the Sahel – a semidesert region south of the Sahara Desert that forms the geographical border between North and West Africa. Much of North Africa consists of a platform of ancient granites and other once-molten rocks, mostly covered by layers of sandstone and limestone. Valuable deposits of iron ore, manganese, oil, phosphates, and natural gas

Saharan Plateau

This vast plateau ranges from 500 to 2,000 ft (150–600 m) high and occupies much of North Africa. "Sahara" is literally the Arabic word for desert and the Saharan Plateau contains most of the world's largest desert – the Sahara – which stretches across virtually the whole width of North Africa. The Sahara has three main types of landscape. *Erg* are areas of deep, rolling sand dunes. *Reg* are vast spreads of gravel and pebbles. *Hammada* are

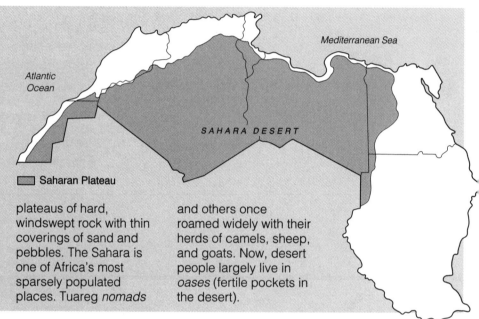

plateaus of hard, windswept rock with thin coverings of sand and pebbles. The Sahara is one of Africa's most sparsely populated places. Tuareg *nomads* and others once roamed widely with their herds of camels, sheep, and goats. Now, desert people largely live in *oases* (fertile pockets in the desert).

Mountains

North Africa has three main mountain areas. Largest and highest is the Atlas Mountain range, which reaches up to 13,600 ft (4,100 m) high and is nearly 2,000 miles (3,200 km) long, stretching across Algeria, Morocco, and Tunisia. Its parallel chains of peaks are mainly sediments rucked up when Africa moved north toward Europe in prehistoric times. Volcanic outflows helped build the two other groups: the Ahaggar Mountains of southeast

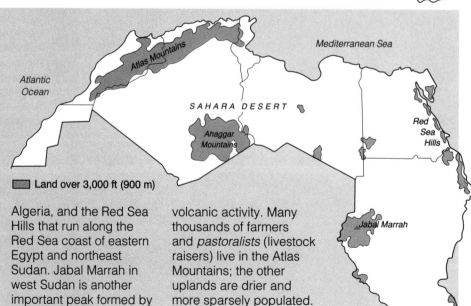

Algeria, and the Red Sea Hills that run along the Red Sea coast of eastern Egypt and northeast Sudan. Jabal Marrah in west Sudan is another important peak formed by volcanic activity. Many thousands of farmers and *pastoralists* (livestock raisers) live in the Atlas Mountains; the other uplands are drier and more sparsely populated.

occur in the northwest and north. Apart from a narrow, low coastal strip, most of the land consists of dry plateaus more than 500 ft (150 m) high with mountain ranges in the northwest and partly volcanic mountains in the south and east. The only large river in North Africa is the Nile – the longest river in the world at 4,145 miles (6,671 km). Densely populated regions include the fertile Nile Valley, the Mediterranean and Atlantic coastal lowlands, and the Atlas Mountains.

Coastal lowlands

Coastal lowlands form the narrow western and northern rim of North Africa. Large tracts of the Atlantic and Mediterranean coasts have low, sandy shores. Hills and cliffs interrupt these lowlands where the Atlas Mountains meet the sea. Most Moroccans inhabit the plains and plateaus that face the Atlantic, while most of the populations of Algeria, Tunisia, and Libya live close to the Mediterranean coast. Moroccan fishing ports support sardine and tuna fisheries and fish-canning factories. Morocco and Tunisia also have many beach resorts.

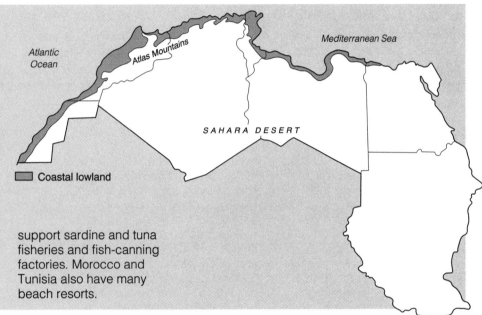

Nile Basin

The Nile Basin is the land drained by the Nile River. Much of the basin lies in the Sahara Desert. The Nile rises in East Africa and flows north to Egypt. In southern Sudan, the Nile meanders through a large, seasonally swampy region called the Sudd before receiving its major tributaries. The river then enters the huge Lake Nasser – created by Egypt's Aswan High Dam. The Nile continues north through Egypt to the Nile Delta, a great apron of silt dumped by the river in the Mediterranean. Before the Aswan High Dam was built in the 1960s, the Nile annually deposited fertile silt on the delta and in the valley when it flooded. The dam ended the annual floods, however, and trapped the silt in Lake Nasser. Nevertheless, the Nile Valley and the Nile Delta remain among the most fertile, and hence densely populated, places in the world.

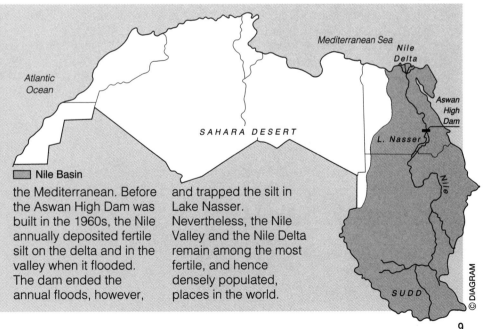

Climate

The climate of North Africa varies from tropical to subtropical according to the latitude and the presence or absence of moist, rain-bearing winds. The region's south lies in the tropics but most of the rest lies north of the Tropic of Cancer. The coastal regions have a subtropical climate with mainly hot, dry summers and mild winters with light to moderate rain. A strip of land south of this region has a semiarid climate with large daily swings in temperature and light rainfall. The Sahara Desert has an arid climate that is largely hot and dry. The desert regions experience scorching summers and mild winters, with great swings of temperature between day and night all year round. Rain is scarce at any time in the Sahara.

Winds

Between November and April, air pressure is higher over the Sahara Desert than over regions to its south. This pressure difference tends to make winds blow outward to the southwest from the west and southward up the Nile River. Meanwhile, depressions moving over the Mediterranean Sea cause winds to blow from west to east along the northern coast of North Africa. From May to October, air pressure is lower over the Sahara than over regions to the north or south, so winds blow mainly inward. Strong local winds include Libya's *sirocco*, Algeria's *simoom*, and Egypt's *khamsin*. These fierce, hot, desert winds can wither plants and whip up stinging clouds of dust and sand that get into buildings, clothes, and into people's eyes, noses, and mouths.

Temperature

The Sahara Desert has hotter summers and cooler winters than regions farther south. In summer, unbroken sunshine beating down from almost directly overhead makes the Sahara one of the hottest places on Earth. The world's highest-ever temperature of 58 °C (136 °F) was measured in the Sahara in Libya, in 1922. At night, however, desert temperatures can plunge to 4.4 °C (40 °F) and frosts are not unknown in winter. Many Saharan people wear heavy clothing to protect themselves from both the heat and the cold. The western and northern coasts of North Africa have less marked seasonal extremes. Southern Sudan is usually warm or hot. Mountain regions tend to be cooler and moister than the lowland areas that surround them.

Rainfall

Most of North Africa is dry or very dry. Only the northwest and southeast get much rain. Annual rainfall ranges from 0.6 in. (1.5 cm) in parts of the Sahara to more than 60 in. (152 cm) in the mountainous regions of Algeria. In the northwest, most rain falls from November through April – when moist depressions move east over the Mediterranean. Winter blizzards can block passes high up in the Atlas Mountains. In the southeast, the wettest time is May through October when moist air moves north from the equator. The Saharan Plateau, and therefore the Sahara Desert, stays almost rainless because it lies under a dry air mass. The rain that does fall usually comes in sudden, short-lived, localized storms that can cause severe flash floods.

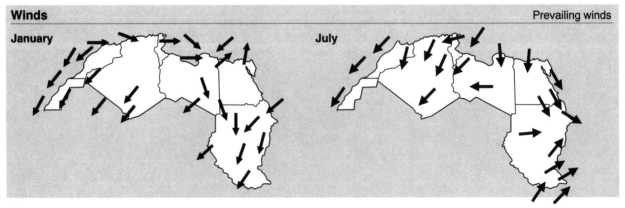

Winds — Prevailing winds

January | July

Temperature   Actual surface temperature

January

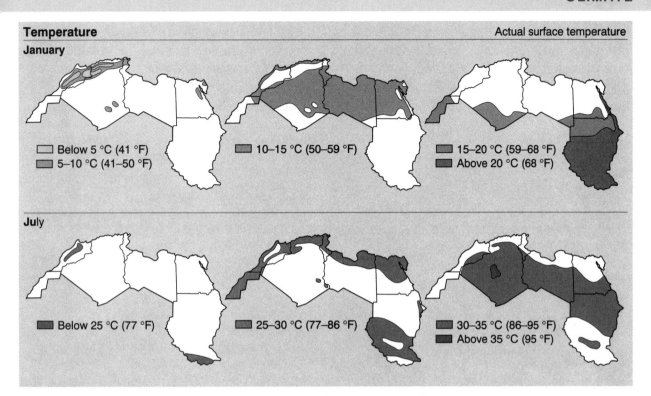

☐ Below 5 °C (41 °F)	☐ 10–15 °C (50–59 °F)	☐ 15–20 °C (59–68 °F)
☐ 5–10 °C (41–50 °F)		☐ Above 20 °C (68 °F)

July

☐ Below 25 °C (77 °F)	☐ 25–30 °C (77–86 °F)	☐ 30–35 °C (86–95 °F)
		☐ Above 35 °C (95 °F)

Rainfall   Total rainfall

November to April

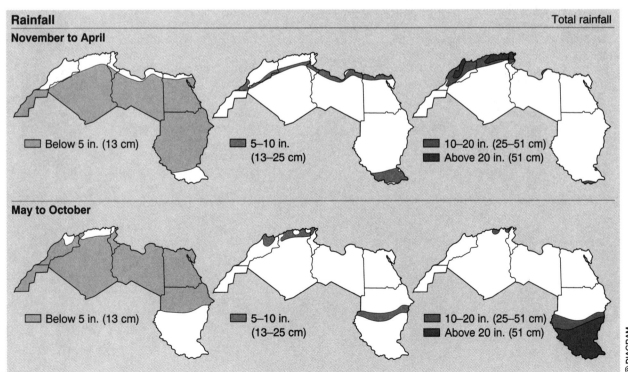

☐ Below 5 in. (13 cm)	☐ 5–10 in. (13–25 cm)	☐ 10–20 in. (25–51 cm)
		☐ Above 20 in. (51 cm)

May to October

☐ Below 5 in. (13 cm)	☐ 5–10 in. (13–25 cm)	☐ 10–20 in. (25–51 cm)
		☐ Above 20 in. (51 cm)

© DIAGRAM

11

Vegetation

The vegetation of North Africa reflects local differences in temperature, rainfall, soil, and the type of underlying rock. *Drought*-adapted plants – long-rooted shrubs and trees that can tap moisture from deep underground – live in the Sahara Desert and its fringing *steppe* (open plain) and semidesert areas. The Mediterranean coast supports areas of dense *scrub* (tracts of scraggly, stunted trees and shrubs) with oak woods and cedar forests in the Atlas Mountains.

Desert

	Typical plants
	1 Acacia
	2 Date palm
	3 Barley

A vast belt of desert vegetation stretches almost right across North Africa. In the Sahara, only plants adapted to long, hot droughts can survive. Small shrubs and low, thorny acacia trees put down deep roots to reach underground moisture. Leaves reduced to spines have small surface areas that limit the amount of water lost through evaporation. Certain plants store water and food in underground bulbs. The seeds of short, hard grasses persist in the soil for years, sprouting quickly after rain to form short-lived pastures. Lines of tamarisks (small trees with slender branches), oleanders (evergreen shrubs), euphorbias (cactuslike shrubs and trees), and other small trees and shrubs mark the course of *wadis* (dry *watercourses*). In oases, date palms rise above citrus-fruit trees that shade vegetable plots, while grains such as barley, millet, and wheat thrive in the open. Cotton is a major cash crop in the irrigated Nile Valley, which has vegetation similar to the oases.

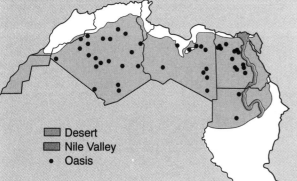

- ▨ Desert
- ▨ Nile Valley
- • Oasis

Steppe and semidesert

	Typical plants
	1 Short grass
	2 Gum arabic acacia
	3 Doum palm

North of the Sahara lies a belt of semidesert and dry grassland where pastures spring up after the seasonal rains. In the grasslands, some palm trees, such as the doum palm, can be found. Large clay basins with salty soil also lie in these regions. The only plants that can grow in these basins are salt-adapted species such as sea rushes and sea lavender. Another belt of semidesert – the Sahel – and dry grassland crosses the middle of Sudan, where grass and scrub grow. Before many people took to settled living, the inhabitants of the northern Sahara moved north in summer to graze their animals on the upland steppes and spent winter in the desert harvesting crops in the oases. People also gather and sell *gum arabic,* which oozes from cuts made in certain acacia trees. It is used to make perfumes and adhesives. The fragile semideserts, especially the Sahel, are prone to *desertification* (becoming desertlike) due to overuse and lack of rainfall.

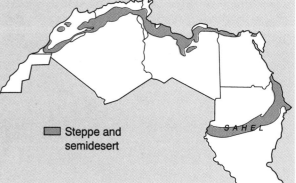

- ▨ Steppe and semidesert

S A H E L

Tropical *savanna* (grasslands with scattered trees and shrubs) dominates the southeast. People have modified the natural vegetation, however. The felling of trees and overgrazing by animals have replaced large tracts of forest with steppe and scrub in the northwest. Crops are grown on coastal lowlands, *oases* (fertile pockets in the desert), and irrigated lands – mainly in the Nile Valley.

Tropical savanna

In North Africa, this mixture of grassland with trees occurs only in the southeast – in the southern half of Sudan. Trees that seasonally shed their leaves predominate in the moist woodland savannas of Sudan's far southwest. Baobab trees thrive on hot, grassy plains as they are able to store water in their thick trunks. Other species include Sudan mahogany and tamarinds (tropical evergreen trees). Pulp taken from the seed pods of tamarinds can be used in cooking or made into a refreshing drink. Tall grasses such as wild sorghum also grow in these regions. The drier parts of southern Sudan have woodland savanna with acacia trees and tracts of land where the chief plants are just short grasses. This region contains the Sudd, a seasonally swampy area where reeds, floating plants, and *papyrus* (tall, reedlike plants) clog the sluggish waterways. Each year grass sprouts on low ground as the floods recede.

Typical plants
1 Baobab
2 Wild sorghum
3 Papyrus

1

2

3

Forest and maquis

Sizable forests flourish chiefly in the northwest of North Africa, mainly on the moist upper levels of the Atlas Mountains. Oaks and conifers (cone-bearing trees such as pines) thrive on the wetter northern and western slopes; evergreen oaks and junipers occur above 3,000 ft (900 m) and cedar forests above 5,000 ft (1,500 m). Deforested by animals and humans, the lower slopes are mostly *maquis* (a mixture of brush and small trees). Broom, gorse, laurel, myrtle, lavender, wild olive, and other maquis plants have narrow and spiny or thick and waxy leaves that cut down water loss to help them to endure the hot summer droughts. On limestone bedrock, maquis gives way to *garigue* (heath and poor scrub with patches of bare rock and soil). On most of the northwest's low coastal plains and valleys, wheat fields and olive groves now occupy the land where trees and forests once grew.

Typical plants
1 Atlas cedar
2 Cork oak
3 Wild olive
4 Lavender

1

2

3

4

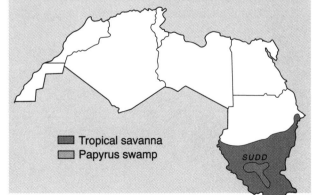

Tropical savanna
Papyrus swamp
SUDD

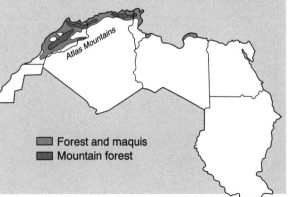

Atlas Mountains
Forest and maquis
Mountain forest

Wildlife

Northwestern North Africa belongs to the *Palearctic faunal realm,* which is a biogeographical zone that also includes Europe and Northern Asia. Therefore, many similar species live in all three areas. For example, red deer, red foxes, and wild boar occur in both northwestern North Africa and Europe. White storks and many small shorebirds winter on North Africa's coasts and marshes but fly north in spring to nest in Europe and Asia – each year millions of birds fly over the Mediterranean Sea. A largely different set of creatures lives in

Desert

Desert wildlife is adapted to the hot, dry environment. The fennec (desert fox) and desert hedgehog both have large ears that radiate heat, helping to keep them cool. Small rodents called jerboas bound over open spaces on their long hind legs. Smaller creatures tend to hide from the Sun's heat by day and feed at night. Larger mammals such as the addax (a large antelope with twisted horns), scimitar oryx (a large antelope with curved horns), and the sand gazelle (a small antelope with backward-pointing horns) have been hunted almost to extinction. Birds range from the houbara bustard (a large bird as tall as a turkey) to small species such as the hoopoe and the desert warbler. Reptiles include the spiny-tailed lizard and sand viper. *Invertebrates* (animals without backbones) include ant lions (meat-eating insects), beetles, scorpions, and desert locusts.

Typical animals
1 Addax
2 Sand gazelle
3 Fennec
4 Desert hedgehog
5 Egyptian jerboa
6 Houbara bustard
7 Hoopoe
8 Spiny-tailed lizard
9 Desert locust

Steppe and semidesert

In the semideserts and *steppes* (open plains) that fringe the desert, creatures that can cope with the dry conditions are found – including some desert species. Large mammals include two kinds of antelope: the addax and the scimitar oryx. The most plentiful small mammals are rodents such as jerboas, gerbils, and the ground squirrels known as susliks. All three are prey to vipers and buzzards. Among the birds, cream-colored coursers eat flies and beetles, while larks and wheatears (a small thrush with long legs) feed on seeds and insects. The short-toed eagle feeds mainly on snakes. Ostriches, the tallest birds in the world, also live in the plains as well as the desert. Insects include desert locusts, beetles, and butterflies. Overhunting has almost wiped out many larger animals in North Africa, though some specimens have been reintroduced.

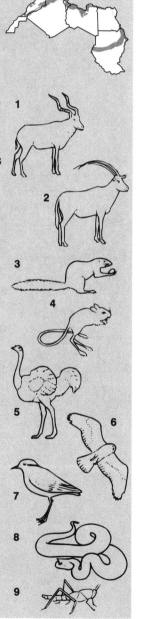

Typical animals
1 Addax
2 Scimitar oryx
3 Suslik
4 Egyptian jerboa
5 Ostrich
6 Short-toed eagle
7 Cream-colored courser
8 Horned desert viper
9 Desert locust

southern Sudan, however, as it is part of the *Ethiopian faunal realm* – a biogeographical zone that includes most of sub-Saharan Africa. Mammals of the Ethiopian realm include lions, antelopes, giraffes, and elephants. Human hunters, herders, and farmers have displaced or decimated many of these wild animal populations throughout North Africa. Over vast stretches of land, cattle, camels, sheep, and goats now graze where antelopes and ostriches once roamed.

Forest and maquis

The mountain forests and shrubby *maquis* of the northwest support a rich variety of animals. Hardy, tailless monkeys called Barbary apes climb high among the cedar trees. The meat-eating, short-legged genets are also agile climbers. On the forest floor, red deer – the only deer in Africa – nibble trees and shrubs; wild boars root for acorns; crested porcupines eat roots and bulbs; and red foxes hunt small mammals. Among the woodland birds, booted eagles prey upon birds, small mammals, and reptiles, and great spotted woodpeckers prise insects from decaying wood. The shrubby maquis conceals warblers, rodents, and reptiles – including snakes and the Mediterranean chameleon. Among the invertebrates are cicadas, praying mantises, and giant peacock moths as big as an adult's hand.

Typical animals
1 Barbary ape
2 Red deer
3 Wild boar
4 Genet
5 Booted eagle
6 Great spotted woodpecker
7 Montpellier snake
8 Mediterranean chameleon
9 Giant peacock moth

Nile Basin

Large grazing mammals of the Nile Basin once included the wild ass, elephant, giraffe, and various antelopes. Large predators were the lion, leopard, cheetah, spotted hyena, and African hunting dog. The hippopotamus once lived in the Nile as far north as Egypt. Smaller beasts still commonly found include the warthog, aardvark (a nocturnal, ant-eating mammal), honey badger, serval (a wildcat), Egyptian mongoose (a short-legged, catlike mammal), and the Egyptian spiny mouse. Bustards, coursers, larks, and the occasional ostrich are birds of dry areas. Warblers and weaver birds live in the woods and the storklike shoebill lives in the swampy Sudd region of southern Sudan. The Nile crocodile and Nile monitor (a flesh-eating lizard) are two of the region's largest reptiles. Termites, beetles, and ants are typical invertebrates.

Typical animals
1 African wild ass
2 Roan antelope
3 Cheetah
4 Egyptian mongoose
5 Egyptian spiny mouse
6 Black-headed weaver
7 Shoebill
8 Nile crocodile
9 Fungus-grower termite

In about 2600 BCE, King Huni begins construction of the first "true" – smooth-sided – Egyptian pyramid, at Maidum. It is completed by Huni's successor, King Snofru.

An ancient oil lamp from Nubia. Nubian kingdoms flourished along the Nile River in present-day Sudan over two thousand years ago.

Cleopatra, who rules Egypt from 47–30 BCE, is the last of the Ptolemaic dynasty. The Ptolemies were of Macedonian (Greek) origin and ruled Egypt from 304 through 30 BCE.

NORTH AFRICAN EVENTS

WORLD EVENTS

Countries or locations in parentheses give the modern-day locations of the states. Dates of independence appear in a table after the chronology.

to 1000 BCE

NORTH AFRICAN EVENTS	WORLD EVENTS
c. 4500 Predynastic Egypt emerges (Nile River)	**c. 3500** Wheel and plow invented
c. 4000 Predynastic Nubia emerges (Egypt/Sudan)	**c. 3500–2300** Sumerian Civilization (Iraq). Founding of Troy
c. 3200 Nubian Kingdom of Kush emerges (Egypt/Sudan)	
c. 3100 Egyptian dynasty established	**c. 3000–1500** Indus Valley Civilization (India/Pakistan)
c. 3000 Berbers settled on coastal region (from Morocco to Egypt)	
c. 2560 Great Pyramid of Khufu (Cheops) and Sphinx built (Egypt)	**c. 1600–1200** Greek Mycenaean Civilization
c. 1500 Kush conquered by Egypt	
c. 1300 Temples of Ramses II and Nefertari built (Egypt)	**c. 1200** Beginning of Judaism

1001 BCE – 1 CE

NORTH AFRICAN EVENTS	WORLD EVENTS
c. 920 Kingdom of Nubia emerges (Egypt/Sudan)	**776** First Olympic Games are held in Greece
814 City-state of Carthage founded (near Tunis)	**c. 563–483** Life of Buddha (Nepal) and founding of Buddhism
750 Greek Empire extends to North African coast (Libya)	
671 Assyrian (Iraqi) rule begins in Egypt	**c. 273–232** Reign of great Indian emperor Ashoka, who unites much of India for the first time
651 Assyrian rule ends in Egypt	
525 Persia (Iran) conquers Egypt	
332 Macedonian (Greek) rule in Egypt	
304 Ptolemaic dynasty founded by Ptolemy (Egypt)	**510** Republic of Rome established
c. 300s Kingdom of Nubia transfers capital to Meroe city (Sudan)	**334–329** Alexander the Great expands Macedonian (Greek) Empire
264– 146 Three Punic Wars between Rome and Carthage	
c. 250 Three Berber kingdoms established on northwest coast	**c. 300** Great Wall begun (China) to keep out Huns to north
146 Romans destroy Carthage	
100 Camels introduced to North Africa	
30 Ptolemaic Empire conquered by Romans	

1–1000

NORTH AFRICAN EVENTS	WORLD EVENTS
285 Romans abandon much of African empire on northwest coast	**c. 30** Jesus of Nazareth crucified
324 Meroitic Kingdom conquered by Axumite Kingdom	**c. 300** Rise of Mayan Civilization
429 Vandals (Europeans) begin conquest of north coast	**455** Vandals sack Rome
533 Vandals conquered by Byzantine (East Roman) Empire	**622** Muhammad's flight to Medina

NORTH AFRICAN EVENTS		WORLD EVENTS
640	Arabs begin conquest of North Africa; Islam introduced	**624** T'ang dynasty unites China
711	Arabs control all of North Africa	**700s** Printing begins to spread from China. Viking raids begin in Europe
789	Independent Arab dynasties begin to emerge	
969	Fatimid dynasty reunites North Africa under Arab rule	

1001–1500

1054	Berber Almoravid dynasty founded (Western Sahara)	**1066** Normans conquer England
1069	Almoravids conquer Morocco	**c. 1150** Angkor Wat built in Cambodia
1147	Berber Almohad dynasty founded (Western Sahara)	**1206** Genghis Khan begins Mongol conquest of Asia
1150	Almoravid Empire collapses; succeeded by Almohads	
1169	Collapse of Fatimid Empire	**1346–49** "Black Death" ravages much of Europe
1269	Collapse of Almohad Empire	
1250	Mamluk rule in Egypt begins; Egypt becomes center of eastern Arab world	**1368** Ming dynasty begins in China
1400s	Funj herders migrate north from the Blue Nile (Sudan)	**1492** Columbus discovers New World

1501–1700

1505	Funj Kingdom founded (Sudan)	**1519–22** Magellan's circumnavigation of the world. Hernan Cortés conquers the Aztecs
1517	Mamluks conquered by Ottoman (Turkish) Empire	
1551	Ottomans conquer Tripoli (Libya)	
1574	Ottomans control most of North Africa except Morocco	
c. 1600	Darfur established (Sudan)	**1619** First African slaves arrive in Jamestown, Virginia
1670	Alawid rule begins (Morocco)	
1700s	Funj Kingdom at greatest extent	

1701–1900

1750	Darfur expands to south and east	**1776–83** American War of Independence
1798	Napoleon, Emperor of France, conquers Egypt	
1801	Ottoman and British forces take Egypt from France	**1789–99** French Revolution
1805	Egypt independent	**1807** Britain outlaws slave trade
1821	Egyptians destroy Funj Kingdom	
1842	French rule begins in Algeria	**1845–51** "Potato Famine" in Ireland
1874	Egypt annexes Darfur	
1881	French rule begins in Tunisia	**1848** Marx and Engels publish *Communist Manifesto*
1882	British rule begins in Egypt; Anglo-Egyptian force conquers Sudan; Mahdi begins campaigns	
1885	Spanish Río de Oro colony established (Western Sahara)	**1861–5** US Civil War
1869	Suez Canal opened (Egypt)	**1865** US abolishes slavery

Between 1086 and 1106, the Islamic Almoravid Empire of North Africa conquers southern Spain.

Muhammad Ali, *pasha* (military leader) of Egypt from 1805–48, acts as an independent ruler retaining only nominal allegiance to the Ottoman Sultan.

Muhammad Ahmad – the "Mahdi" – and his forces create a powerful Islamic, state by 1885 in what is now Sudan.

© DIAGRAM

17

During World War II, the Egyptian Camel Corps fights alongside the Allies in the desert against the German army.

Gamal Abd an-Nasser takes power in Egypt in 1954. His nationalization of the Suez Canal in 1956 leads to French, British, and Israeli forces invading the country.

Egyptian stamp showing the Aswan High Dam on the Nile; it is begun in 1960 and becomes fully operational in 1970.

NORTH AFRICAN EVENTS		WORLD EVENTS
1889	Mahdist State at greatest extent	**1871** German
1898	Anglo-Egyptian forces conquer Mahdists. Darfur independent	Empire proclaimed
1901–1950		
1911	Italy conquers Libya	**1905** First Russian
1912	French rule begins in Morocco	Revolution
1914	All North Africa under foreign rule	**1914–18** World
1914–	World War I; Egypt used as a	War I (WWI)
1918	British military base; parts of	**1917** US enters
	Egypt and Sudan ceded to	WWI. Second
	Italian Libya	Russian Revolution;
1916	Anglo-Egyptian Sudan	socialism adopted
	absorbs Darfur	**1929** Wall Street
1925	Huge irrigated farming project	Crash in US
	begun in Gezira (Sudan)	**1930s** Worldwide
1939–	World War II; many major battles	depression
1945	fought in North Africa; Allied	**1939–45** World
	forces take Libya from Italy	War II (WWII)
1945	The Arab League, an organization	**1941** US enters WWII
	of Arab states, is founded	**1950–3** Korean War
1951–1960		
1951	Libya declared an independent	**1954** French
	monarchy under King Idris I	defeated in Vietnam
1952	Military coup in Egypt ousts king	**1955** Warsaw Pact
1953	Egypt's king deposed by military	signed by
1954	Military coup in Egypt; Gamal Abd	communist East
	an-Nasser becomes head of state	Europe
1955	Civil war in Sudan between	**1956** Soviet troops
	northerners and southerners	crush Hungarian
1956	French and Spanish Morocco	uprising
	unified; Alawid dynasty in power	**1957** North and
1956–	Israel, France, and Britain invade	South Vietnam
1957	Egypt during Suez Crisis	at war
1960	Organization of Petroleum	**1959** Cuban
	Exporting Companies (OPEC)	revolution led by
	forms to unite oil exporters	Fidel Castro
1961–1970		
1960s	Aswan High Dam built in Egypt,	**1961** Berlin Wall
	creating the huge Lake Nasser	goes up
1961	Libya starts exporting oil	**1963** US president
1963	Organization of African Unity	J.F. Kennedy is
	(OAU) founded	assassinated
1965	Military coup in Algeria led by	**1965–73** US
	Colonel Houari Boumedienne	involvement in
1967	Six-Day War between Egypt	Vietnam War
	and Israel	**1967–70** Biafran
1969	Military coup in Libya led by	(Nigerian Civil) War
	Colonel Muammar al Qaddafi.	**1969** Neil Armstrong
	Military coup in Sudan	is first man on Moon

NORTH AFRICAN EVENTS		WORLD EVENTS
1970	Nasser dies; succeeded by Colonel Anwar Sadat	**1970** Brief civil war in Jordan

1971–1980

1971	Libya begins to nationalize foreign oil company holdings	**1973** Oil Crisis after Arabs ban oil sales to the US
1972	End of first Sudanese civil war; south granted regional autonomy	**1974** "Watergate" scandal in US. Portuguese Revolution
1973	Yom Kippur War between Egypt and Israel	
1975	Western Sahara ceded to Morocco and Mauritania by Spain	**1975** Communists reunite Vietnam
1976	Libya involved in unsuccessful coup attempt in Sudan. Western Saharan guerrillas launch anti-Moroccan offensive. Multiparty elections in Egypt	**1975–9** Khmer Rouge reign of terror in Cambodia
1977	Four-day war between Libya and Egypt	**1978–9** Iranian revolution
1978	Death of Boumedienne. Strikes and protests turn into large-scale rioting in Tunisia	**1979** Civil wars in Nicaragua and El Salvador
1979	Camp David talks end state of war between Egypt and Israel	**1979–89** USSR in Afghanistan
1980	Libyan troops sent to Chad	**1980–8** Iran-Iraq War: US backs Iraq

1981–1990

1981	Casablanca Massacre in Morocco. Sadat is assassinated; Hosni Mubarak succeeds him	**1982** Falklands War between UK and Argentina
1983	Sudan adopts *Sharia* (Islamic holy) law against wishes of non-Muslim south; civil war breaks out	**1982–5** Israeli invasion of Lebanon
1984	First free elections in Egypt	**1986** Chernobyl nuclear accident in USSR. "Iran-Contra" scandal breaks in US
1985	OAU admits Western Saharan representatives; Morocco leaves OAU. Military coup in Sudan	
1986	US bombs Tripoli, Libya. Elections end military rule in Sudan	
1988–1989	Economic hardship causes civil unrest to escalate in Algeria	**1989** Revolution in Romania. Massacre in Tiananmen Square, Beijing, China. US invasion of Panama. Berlin Wall demolished
1989	Libyan military aircraft shot down by US. Opposition parties legalized in Algeria. Multiparty elections in Tunisia. Military coup in Sudan. Union of Arab Maghreb (UAM) founded	
1990	Famine in Sudan threatens 8,000,000 people. 50,000 Berbers demonstrate in Algeria after Berber language is outlawed	**1990** Gulf War begins after Iraq invades Kuwait. East and West Germany reunited Breakup of USSR.

The Egyptian army is heavily defeated in the Yom Kippur War against Israel in 1973.

Anwar Sadat, Egyptian president, makes peace with Israel at the Camp David talks in 1979; he is assassinated in 1981.

In the 1980s and 1990s, drought and civil strife cause hundreds of thousands of refugees to pour into Sudan from Ethiopia, Chad, and elsewhere. The civil war in Sudan prevents relief supplies reaching the refugees and famine results.

© DIAGRAM

Muammar al Qaddafi, Libyan leader since 1969, has proved to be a controversial figure in international politics.

Fearing the popularity of radical Islamic fundamentalists, the Algerian government cancels the second round of multiparty elections in 1991. Rioting follows and radical Muslim fundamentalists battle with pro-government death squads.

NORTH AFRICAN EVENTS	WORLD EVENTS
1991–1996	
1991 US and British courts blame Libya for terrorist attacks on civilian airplanes. Ruling party in Algeria refuses to allow second round of legislative elections to be held after losing to radical Front d'Islamic Salvation (FIS) in the first; FIS is banned. Cease-fire in Western Sahara	End of apartheid in South Africa. Civil war breaks out in Somalia. End of Gulf War. Breakup of Yugoslavia; war erupts in Slovenia and Croatia
1992 UN's demand that Libya turns over suspected terrorists is refused; sanctions are imposed. Rioting in Algeria and president is assassinated; military coup	Cold War ends. Riots in LA. War in former Yugoslavia spreads to Bosnia
1993 Islamic militants in Egypt clash with security forces and attack foreign tourists	Israeli-PLO peace agreement
1994 Libya and Chad sign agreement that ends twenty-year border dispute. Islamic militants attack foreigners in Algeria and hijack a French airliner. Algeria's military rulers install retired general Liamine Zeroual as president	Free elections in South Africa. Civil war in Rwanda. Peace in Somalia. US intervention in Haiti. Cease-fire announced by IRA
1995 Zeroual elected president in multiparty elections; Islamic militants continue terror campaign in Algeria and plant bombs in France. Attempted assassination of Mubarak in Ethiopia; Mubarak cracks down on Islamic militants. Government and rebels declare cease-fires in Sudan	Peace in former Yugoslavia. France carries out nuclear tests in Pacific. Assassination of Israeli prime minister. Bomb in Oklahoma city, OK, kills 169 people
1996 Unrest continues in Algeria. Anti-Qaddafi protestors shot dead in Libya. Sudan refuses to hand over three Egyptians accused of attempting to assassinate Mubarak; UN imposes sanctions. Cease-fires in Sudan prove short-lived: fighting continues	IRA end cease-fire. TWA airliner explodes off Long Island, NY, killing 230 passengers and crew

Muslims at prayer in a North African town. Radical Islamic fundamentalism is growing increasingly popular in the 1990s. Radical Muslim groups in Algeria and Egypt, in particular, are employing terrorist tactics and attacking foreigners to further their causes.

COLONIAL OCCUPATION AND INDEPENDENCE

Country	Independence	Occupied *	Colonial powers
Algeria	Jul 3, 1962	1842	France
Egypt	Feb 28, 1922	1798–1801 1882	France Britain
Libya	Dec 24, 1951	1911	Italy
Morocco: (French) (Spanish)	 Mar 2, 1956 Apr 7, 1956	 1912 1912	 France Spain
Sudan	Jan 1, 1956	1898	Under joint British and Egyptian rule
Tunisia	Mar 20, 1956	1881	France
Western Sahara (*as Río de Oro*)	(ceded to Morocco and Mauritania in 1975)	1885	Spain

* The years given for the beginning of colonial occupation of the modern-day nations are those by which a significant area of coastal and hinterland territory had been effectively occupied by a colonial power.

King Idris I becomes the first leader of independent Libya in 1951.

Egypt's nationalization of the Suez Canal is orchestrated by the recently-appointed head of state, Gamal Abd an-Nasser in 1956. Ships are sunk to blockade the canal and despite French, British, and Israeli military intervention, Egypt keeps control of the canal.

In 1986, nearly one hundred years after the Mahdi is defeated by Anglo-Egyptian forces, one of his descendants, Sadiq al Mahdi, becomes prime minister of Sudan.

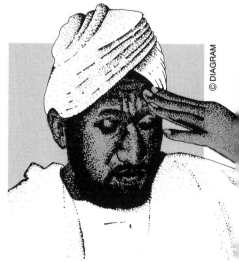

© DIAGRAM

Pictorial history

Key

—— Trade route

Marrakech Modern town or city

The Great Synagogue of Tunis, which was built six hundred years ago. Until the mid-twentieth century, many Jewish people lived in North Africa.

This twelfth-century picture depicts a Moorish naval invasion of Spain. Between the 700s and the 1200s, Muslims from North Africa invaded and conquered southern Spain, where they were known as the "Moors."

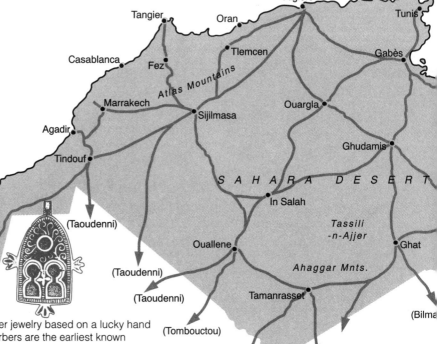

An item of Berber jewelry based on a lucky hand symbol. The Berbers are the earliest known inhabitants of North Africa; they were settled on the Mediterranean coast by 3000 BCE.

A camel *caravan* (company of travelers) crossing the Sahara Desert. Ever since camels were introduced to North Africa about 2,000 years ago, caravans of pack-carrying animals have crisscrossed the desert along well-worn routes.

An eighteenth-century North African Sufi lodge, which would have housed students, guests, and pilgrims. Sufi lodges such as this one were active in spreading Islam throughout North Africa, in particular during the 1700s and 1800s.

A gravestone of an Arab sultan of Morocco dating from the thirteenth century. In 640, Arabs first invaded North Africa from Arabia in southwest Asia; by 711 they had conquered the whole region. The Arabs brought with them their religion, Islam, and their language, Arabic, which now dominate North African culture.

Paintings on the rocks of Tassili-n-Ajjer, Algeria, depict life in the Sahara thousands of years ago, when the desert had rivers, lakes, and a wealth of plant and animal life.

A Carthaginian coin dating from sometime after 400 BCE. Carthage, originally a Phoenician colony on the coast near present-day Tunis, was ruled independently from c. 600 BCE.

For many centuries, goods and people have traveled up and down the Nile on *feluccas*, small, narrow boats propelled by oar or wind.

Of the ten pyramids at Giza, Egypt, the largest is the Great Pyramid of Khufu (or Cheops), which stands roughly 460 ft (140 m) high and was built between 2600 and 2500 BCE. The Ancient Egyptians built many pyramids as tombs for their dead kings and queens.

Egypt's *Coptic* (that is Christian) Period lasted from the 200s to 642 – the date Muslim Arabs conquered Egypt.

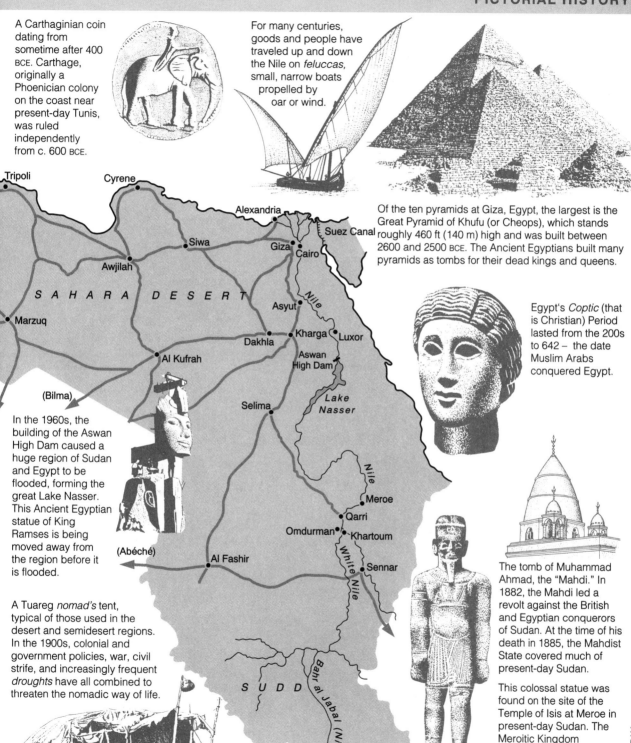

In the 1960s, the building of the Aswan High Dam caused a huge region of Sudan and Egypt to be flooded, forming the great Lake Nasser. This Ancient Egyptian statue of King Ramses is being moved away from the region before it is flooded.

A Tuareg *nomad's* tent, typical of those used in the desert and semidesert regions. In the 1900s, colonial and government policies, war, civil strife, and increasingly frequent *droughts* have all combined to threaten the nomadic way of life.

The tomb of Muhammad Ahmad, the "Mahdi." In 1882, the Mahdi led a revolt against the British and Egyptian conquerors of Sudan. At the time of his death in 1885, the Mahdist State covered much of present-day Sudan.

This colossal statue was found on the site of the Temple of Isis at Meroe in present-day Sudan. The Meroitic Kingdom flourished on the Nile over 2,000 years ago.

© DIAGRAM

23

Distribution of peoples

1 Berbers
Although spread throughout North Africa, the majority of Berbers live in Morocco and Algeria. Although many Berbers live in settled communities, most practice *seminomadic pastorlaism*. The Berbers are Muslims and speak a variety of Berber languages.

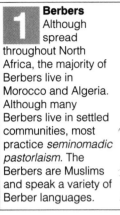

2 Tuareg
The Tuareg (or Kel Tamacheq or Kel Tagelmust) are a *nomadic* Berber people, the so-called "Blue Men" of the Sahara. They can be found throughout North Africa's desert regions and as far south as northern Nigeria. The Tuareg language is called Tamacheq and it has several dialects. Most Tuareg are Muslims.

3 Arabs of North Africa
A people originally from southwest Asia, Arabs are now settled throughout most of North Africa and form its largest ethnic group. The Bedouin are *nomadic* Arabs who are mostly found in the desert regions of Algeria, Libya, and Sudan. Arabic is the language of the Arabs and is the most widely spoken language in North Africa. The vast majority of North African Arabs are Muslims.

4 Copts
The Copts are the Christian minority in Egypt. Although there is a *Coptic* language, it is largely reserved for use in Coptic services and is rarely used on an everyday basis. The vast majority of Copts use Arabic.

5 Dinka
The Dinka are the largest and most widespread group in southern Sudan. The Dinka language is also called Dinka. Although some Dinka have converted to Christianity or Islam, the Dinka religion is still thriving.

Mediterranean Sea

TUNISIA

MOROCCO

ALGERIA

SAHARA

WESTERN SAHARA

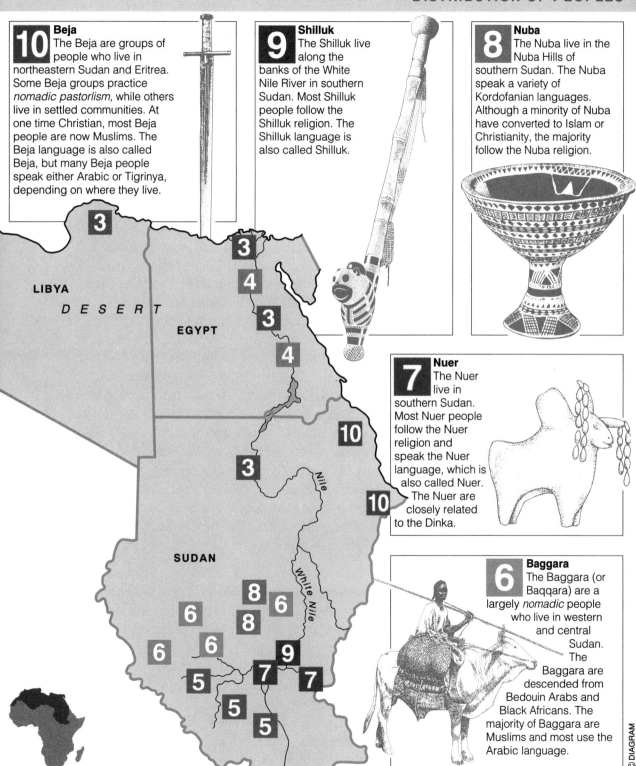

10 Beja
The Beja are groups of people who live in northeastern Sudan and Eritrea. Some Beja groups practice *nomadic pastorlism,* while others live in settled communities. At one time Christian, most Beja people are now Muslims. The Beja language is also called Beja, but many Beja people speak either Arabic or Tigrinya, depending on where they live.

9 Shilluk
The Shilluk live along the banks of the White Nile River in southern Sudan. Most Shilluk people follow the Shilluk religion. The Shilluk language is also called Shilluk.

8 Nuba
The Nuba live in the Nuba Hills of southern Sudan. The Nuba speak a variety of Kordofanian languages. Although a minority of Nuba have converted to Islam or Christianity, the majority follow the Nuba religion.

7 Nuer
The Nuer live in southern Sudan. Most Nuer people follow the Nuer religion and speak the Nuer language, which is also called Nuer. The Nuer are closely related to the Dinka.

6 Baggara
The Baggara (or Baqqara) are a largely *nomadic* people who live in western and central Sudan. The Baggara are descended from Bedouin Arabs and Black Africans. The majority of Baggara are Muslims and most use the Arabic language.

LIBYA

DESERT

EGYPT

SUDAN

Nile

White Nile

© DIAGRAM

Introduction

The peoples of North Africa reflect a wide variety of lifestyles and cultures. This book describes a selected sample of these cultures, where possible detailing contemporary changes and the effects they have had on people's lives.

Historical overview

Egypt is one of the world's oldest civilizations. It developed along the banks of the Nile River about 5,000 years ago. The Ancient Egyptians were great mathematicians, builders, and astronomers. They developed a system of picture writing, called *hieroglyphics*, and a religion based on belief in an afterlife. The first peoples living west of Egypt along the Mediterranean shore were the Berbers, who were in the area the same time that Ancient Egypt was flourishing.

North Africa lies close to southwest Asia and to the countries bordering the north of the Mediterranean Sea, so it has been constantly invaded and occupied by peoples from outside Africa. Greek, Roman, Phoenician, and Ottoman (Turkish) people all invaded from Europe or southwest Asia and colonized parts of North Africa at different times. The biggest change came with the advent of the Arabs, who began invading North Africa in the seventh century, bringing with them their language, Arabic, their culture, and their religion, Islam. The spread of Islam had a profound impact on the peoples of North Africa and their traditions. From the 700s to the late 1400s, first Arab and later Berber Muslims from Morocco, known as "Moors," occupied Spain. In more modern times the British, French, Italians, and Spanish set up colonies and "spheres of influence" along the Mediterranean coast. European colonization greatly affected North Africa, setting the modern political boundaries and triggering violent, nationalistic independence wars such as that in Algeria.

Geography

A knowledge of the geography of North Africa is helpful for understanding the people and their ways of life. North Africa is very different in character from the rest of the continent. The great Sahara Desert, which stretches from the Atlantic Ocean in the west to the Red Sea in the east, effectively divides Africa in two. A fertile strip of land runs along the north and west coasts, bordering the Mediterranean Sea and Atlantic Ocean. South of this strip is a wilderness of sand, gravel, and bare rock, blazing hot by day and bitterly cold at night. This is the Sahara, a name that means "desert" in Arabic. It covers an area of almost 3,500,000 square miles, nearly one-third of Africa.

The Sahara was not always dry. During the last Ice Age, which ended roughly 10,000 years ago, it had a relatively moist climate. Lakes and rivers dotted the land, and there were forests and grasslands where many animals roamed. Then, from about 4000 BCE onward, the Sahara slowly dried out. The natural barrier created by the Sahara is broken only by the Nile, the world's longest river. Its waters have created a narrow, green strip of fertile land that runs from south to north through the desert in Sudan and Egypt. Seven other countries are partly covered by the Sahara: Algeria, Morocco, and Tunisia in North Africa, and Chad, Mali, Mauritania, and Niger in West Africa. South of the Sahara is a narrow strip of semidesert called the Sahel. This region has been subject to a series of severe *droughts* (periods of inadequate rainfall) since the late 1960s. Drought and the overuse of the fragile semidesert lands that fringe the Sahara has turned patches of land into desert – a process called *desertification*.

Oases

Rainfall in the Sahara is unpredictable. Some areas may go several years with no rain at all, while several inches may fall in a few hours at other places. Much of this water evaporates quickly in the fierce heat of the day. Vast reserves of water lie under the Sahara, however, some of which is probably "fossil water" that accumulated underground when the Sahara was still green. These underground water sources provide enough moisture for sparse vegetation to grow along the valleys of long-gone rivers. They also feed springs that create *oases* (patches of lush vegetation in the midst of the desert). Every oasis has a permanent population, which draws on underground water for irrigation to grow crops. Only a few parts of the Sahara have no plant life at all.

People today

The population figures provided for each people are estimates from 1980 to 1996. The ethnic groups selected for inclusion tend to be distributed across more than one country. It is difficult, therefore, to use national censuses (which vary in frequency from nation to nation) to gather up-to-date information about a people's numbers. Statistics have been taken instead from a variety of sociological and anthropological sources – they have been included only as a guide to the size and relative importance of an ethnic group.

The distinction between North Africa and sub-Saharan Africa is not just geographical. The people are also different and geography has

© DIAGRAM

helped to make them so. South of the Sahara, the predominant people are descended from Bantu, Cushitic, or Nilotic ancestors. These three linguistic and cultural groupings comprise the majority population of sub-Saharan Africa – the "Black Africans." Along the Mediterranean coast, the people are descended from Arab, Berber, and Black African ancestors. They belong to a number of ethnic groups and intermarriage, conquest, and migration has led to new forms of ethnic identity. The main groups along the Mediterranean coast today are the Arabs and Berbers. A number of Black African peoples – mostly Nilotic – live in southern Sudan. The Dinka, Nuer, and Shilluk of southern Sudan are Nilotic peoples.

Although some ethnic groups have distinctive ways of life, most people of North Africa are linked by two things: language and religion. The majority of people in all the countries of North Africa speak Arabic, even if it is not their first language, and nearly all follow the religion of Islam, which spread from southwest Asia into North Africa in the seventh century. Many people of southern Sudan, however, are Christians or follow an African religion. Along the Mediterranean shore many people speak a European language as well as Arabic or an African language.

Lifestyles

The population of North Africa is roughly fifty-percent rural. This statistic hides a huge variety of lifestyles. Although many people are farmers; others are traders, scholars, weavers, doctors, artists, writers, teachers, miners – there are as many occupations as you would expect to find in any contemporary society. It is difficult, therefore, to describe the typical lifestyle of any specific group of people. Increasingly, rural people are drawn to the cities to find work as eking out a rural livelihood becomes more difficult. Large cities – some of which are ancient – are concentrated in the north, largely in the countries of the *Maghreb* (Morocco, Algeria, and Tunisia) and Egypt.

Geography plays an important role in both lifestyle and culture. The Nile Valley, the Mediterranean coastlands, and the Atlas Mountains of northwest Africa are fertile regions where the greatest number of people live. Nearly two million people, however, live in the Sahara or on its edges. *Nomadic* peoples, such as some Tuareg, keep flocks of sheep and goats and move from one patch of vegetation to another in the desert in search of pasture and water for their herds. Other desert travelers include traders who carry goods across the Sahara, linking the people of the south with those of the north. Ever since camels were introduced to the Sahara about 2,000 years ago, *caravans* (companies of travelers) with pack-carrying animals have crisscrossed the desert along well-worn trails. In modern times, these routes are now more likely to be traveled by trucks than caravans of camels.

The pattern of life in southern Sudan is slightly different, as the region has both rainy and dry seasons and parts are seasonally swampy. Here, herders practice *seminomadic pastoralism* and move from one place to another according to the season of the year.

Recent developments

The pages that follow often describe the "traditional" ways of life and culture of many of the peoples of North Africa. Neither tradition nor culture is static, however, but each changes to reflect new circumstances or absorb new influences. Some groups are more isolated than others and have experienced less interference from the outside world, while others have adopted nontraditional customs and practices as a result of outside influences. Furthermore, for many years now the people of southern Sudan have been rebelling against the politically dominant north – where the Sudanese government is based. The government's attempts to impose *Sharia* (Islamic holy) law on the largely non-Muslim south triggered the most recent outbreak of hostilities over a decade ago. The government has dealt harshly with the rebels and has since been accused by various international agencies of human rights abuses and attempted genocide (extermination) of peoples such as the Nuba, Nuer, and Dinka.

Throughout North Africa, tourism and the spread of Western-style consumerism have brought changes in dress and other influences. All ethnic groups have been affected by the increasing role played by the now-independent governments of the countries of North Africa. Political strife, desertification, the growth of industry and mineral exploitation, and the desire to confine nomads to permanent settlements so that they can be more easily governed have all taken their toll. Many "traditionally" rural people today combine life in the homestead or village with work on an oil rig or in a refinery, bringing in much-needed money and at the same time changing the way in which livelihoods are made.

In spite of these changes, many groups do retain aspects of their customary ways of life. In fact, such changes in some cases offer an opportunity to develop a modern interpretation of a custom, such as the use of synthetic fabrics in ceremonial costume or the inclusion of imported foods in indigenous dishes.

© DIAGRAM

Arabs of North Africa

Arabs originate from Arabia (present day Saudi Arabia), where millions still live today. Now, however, there are more Arabs in North Africa than in Saudi Arabia. Their occupation of Africa came about as a result of the creation of a new religion, Islam.

Numbering over 100 million, Arabs are the most numerous ethnic group in North Africa. In many countries, Arabs have intermarried with the original people. Most Egyptians are a mixture of Arabs and the descendants of Ancient Egyptians. Nearly 90 percent of Libyans are descended from both Arabs and Berbers, and nearly half of the Sudanese population is Arab. The other North African countries (Morocco, Algeria, and Tunisia) form the *Maghreb* – an Arabic term meaning "the West." Tunisia's population is 98 percent Arab, Algeria's 83 percent, and Morocco's 70 percent.

Arab expansion
After the death of the Prophet Muhammad in 632, his Arab followers began the invasion and conquest of North Africa. These maps show the expansion of Arab peoples in the region. As they gained new territories, the Arabs brought Islam to the region.

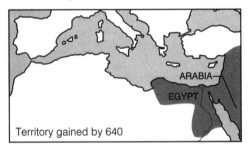

Territory gained by 640

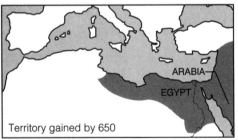

Territory gained by 650

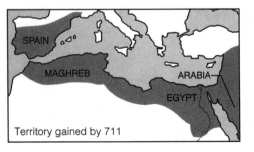

Territory gained by 711

History

An Arab general, Amr ibn al As, led an army 4,000 strong into Egypt in 640, beginning the Arab invasion of North Africa. At that time, Egypt was part of the Byzantine, or East Roman, Empire. In 642, the Byzantines surrendered Egypt to the Arabs. The country came under the rule of governors appointed by the *caliphs*, the rulers of the Arab world. In 670, Uqba ibn Nafi, an Arab general, raided the Barbary Coast, the northwest African territory of the Berbers. By 711, Arabs controlled all of North Africa as well as southern Spain, where they were known as "Moors." The Arabs colonized Cyrenaica and Tripolitania, the coastal regions of what is now Libya, pushing out or absorbing the Berbers who lived there. Many Berbers soon converted to Islam.

Language

The Arabic language is a Semitic language. This is a language group that also includes Hebrew and the Ethiopian languages of Amharic and Tigrinya. There are many different forms of Arabic. Colloquial, or spoken, Arabic comprises all the dialects spoken in different Arabic countries. The Arabic spoken by a Tunisian, for example, is different from that spoken by an Egyptian.

Gravestone
The gravestone of a king of the Marinid dynasty of Morocco, Sultan Abu Yaqub Yusuf, who reigned from 1286–1307. The Arabic inscriptions commemorate the dead king and quote from the *Koran* (Islamic holy book). The stone is made from marble and would have stood at the head of the grave or been embedded in a wall.

Arabs of North Africa timeline	
632	Death of the Prophet Muhammad
640	Arab invasion and conquest of North Africa begins
642	Arabs conquer Egypt
661	Omayyad rule over Arab empire in North Africa begins
710	Omayyad conquest of western *Maghreb* and Spain begins
711	North Africa and southern Spain conquered by Arabs
750	Abbasids overthrow Omayyads
789	Independent Arab dynasties begin to emerge in North Africa
909	Fatimids begin conquest of North Africa
969	Fatimids control North Africa
c. 1000	Fatimids begin to lose North African territories
1069	Berber Almoravid dynasty begins rule in Morocco
1169	Last remaining Fatmids in Egypt overthrown
1200s	Much of North Africa is controlled by Berbers
1250	Mamluk rule in Egypt begins
1510	Some cities under European rule
1517	Ottomans conquer Mamluks
1574	Ottomans control all of North African coast except Morocco
1610	Morocco divides into two warring kingdoms
1670	Morocco reunited by Alawids
1798	Napoleon conquers Egypt
1805	Egypt independent
1914	North Africa under colonial rule
1945	League of Arab States founded
1950s	Many North African countries become independent
1960s	Military coups in both Algeria and Libya
1973	Worldwide oil crisis begins after Arabs impose oil embargo
1990s	Resurgence of Arab nationalism and Islamic militancy in many North African nations

Written Arabic, however, descends directly from the classical language of the *Koran* (Islamic holy book) and is the standard written language of all Arab nations. A spoken form of it – Modern Standard Arabic – is used in broadcasting, films, and for communication between Arabs who would otherwise speak different dialects. Classical Arabic is now only used in the Koran.

Arabic is the official language of Algeria, Egypt, Libya, Morocco, Sudan, and Tunisia. The legacy of French colonialism remains, however, in that French is widely spoken throughout the Maghreb countries. Even since independence, the region's links with France have grown through tourism and migrant labor.

Ways of life

Arab ways of life vary as they are usually influenced by local cultures. About one-third of North African Arabs live and work in cities and towns. The rest are either farmers or herders – such as the widely-scattered Bedouin Arabs. Town life varies. Wealthy Arabs may live in modern houses and work in commerce or in industry. They may shop in modern, Western-style stores. Most urban Arabs, however, live in crowded, older parts of the

© DIAGRAM

Arabic script

Arabic is written from right to left. The Arabic alphabet has twenty-eight symbols, which are mostly consonants. Vowels are shown by diacritics – marks like accents – above or below the letters. These are normally omitted; they are generally only shown in the Classical Arabic of the *Koran* (Islamic holy book) and in elementary schoolbooks.

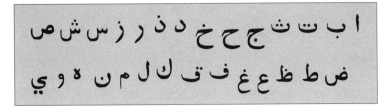

Kufic and Nashki

Arabic script has two main styles, angular Kufic and the more rounded Nashki. Kufic was more popular in the early years of Islam. From the eleventh century onward, Nashki became more frequently used. The example shown uses the Kufic style for a silk tapestry from tenth-century Egypt.

towns, where the streets are often too narrow and winding for vehicles. Many streets are lined with stalls and open-fronted stores where people sell food and make and sell craft products.

Rural Arabs tend to live in small villages. In Egypt, for example, each village has a *mosque* (Islamic house of worship), perhaps a bathhouse, and a few stores. Some Arabs have their own plots of land, but many have to work for large, wealthy landowners growing cash crops such as grapes, dates, cotton, cereals, and citrus fruits.

ECONOMY In the twentieth century, the discovery of oil and mineral deposits in many North African countries has enriched Arab economies. For example, Libya, Egypt, and Algeria are now major oil exporters; Morocco and Tunisia have some of the world's largest supplies of phosphates, which are used in fertilizers.

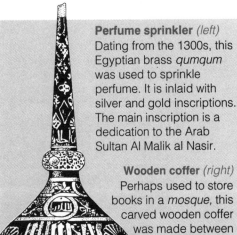

Perfume sprinkler (left)
Dating from the 1300s, this Egyptian brass *qumqum* was used to sprinkle perfume. It is inlaid with silver and gold inscriptions. The main inscription is a dedication to the Arab Sultan Al Malik al Nasir.

Wooden coffer (right)
Perhaps used to store books in a *mosque,* this carved wooden coffer was made between 1300 and 1500. The style of the Arabic inscriptions suggests that it was made in Fez, Morocco.

Manufacturing industries have also been developed: Algeria, Libya, and Tunisia are all major concrete manufacturers and Egypt exports cotton cloth. Inevitably, these industries have affected the lifestyles of many Arabs in North Africa – bringing new job opportunities and greater affluence to some.

BEDOUIN The Bedouin are an Arab subgroup who are chiefly *nomadic pastoralists* – they travel with their herds of sheep, goats, and camels in search of water and pasture. The Bedouin are mostly found in and around the Sahara Desert. Algeria, Libya, and Sudan have the greatest number of Bedouin. The Bedouin still use camels as their main form of desert transportation, but the great camel *caravans* (companies of travelers) of the past are being steadily replaced by trucks.

Social structure

The family is the most important part of Arab society. Arranged marriages are common, but gradually more young people are choosing their own partners. Men tend to be the heads of Arab households. They go out to work or work in the fields, while the women work in the home. Few women have jobs after they marry. In some parts, however, and especially in cities, women are able to work outside the home and hold responsible jobs. Men and women usually eat separately and sometimes pray separately as well – the women at home if they are not allowed into the local mosque. For social contact, women visit neighbors, friends, and relatives in their own homes. Egyptian women tend to have more freedom than in other parts of the Arab world, although the recent rise in radical Islamic fundamentalism threatens to reverse this.

Culture and religion

RELIGION The vast majority of Arabs are Muslims. Islam was founded in 622 by Muhammad – an Arab religious leader who lived in what is now Saudi Arabia. Muhammad is revered throughout the Islamic world as the Prophet of Allah. Islam united the Arab peoples, and it inspired them, after Muhammad's death in 632, to spread the new religion. Islam was the driving force behind the Arab invasion and conquest of North Africa.

Clothing
Arab men in cities generally wear Western-style clothes, but often cover a formal suit with a *jalabiya* (a loose, cotton robe).

Arab town
The *medina* is the old section of an Arab town, and often has narrow winding streets. Part of it is always the *souk,* a marketplace.

© DIAGRAM

Islam in North Africa

Within four centuries of the Arab conquest of North Africa, which was completed by 711, the great majority of the region's inhabitants had converted to Islam — the religion practiced by Muslims. Islam is also practiced widely throughout the rest of Africa.

Islam is a monotheistic *religion (believing in one God) in which the universe, and all within it, are the creation of* Allah *who is considered all-powerful, just, and merciful. Islam is very much a communal and practical religion; more than just a moral code, it includes laws that affect all aspects of life. Most North Africans are* Sunni Muslims, *and Sunnis make up about 85–90 percent of all Muslims worldwide. Sunnis place less emphasis on the importance of a religious hierarchy led by* imams *(spiritual leaders) than do other Muslims.*

Conflicts have existed for some time in North Africa between fundamental Muslims and believers in secular (nonreligious) ideals of government. In recent years, these conflicts have combined with economic and social crises — most notably in Algeria and Egypt — to lead to violent outbursts by radical Islamic fundamentalists, seeking the creation of states

Pottery design *(left)*
Text from the *Koran* (Islamic holy book) is sometimes inscribed on North African pottery, such as this Tunisian pot. It is also common for potters to paint an image that only resembles Koranic script. This is to prevent Koranic writings from being used for unholy purposes – to decorate a pot that is used to hold alcohol, for example.

governed by Sharia *(Islamic holy) law, a detailed code of conduct enforced in law. In Sudan, Sharia law was imposed in 1983. Opposition to Sharia law was a major force in the civil war that has split Sudan into rival north and south factions.*

The Prophet Muhammad and the Koran

Muslims believe Muhammad to have been the last messenger of God, completing the sacred teachings of Abraham and Moses, the Jewish prophets of the Old Testament, and Jesus. It was through the Prophet Muhammad that the teachings of Islam were revealed. Muslims often say or write "Peace be upon Him" whenever they refer to Muhammad.

Muhammad was born in Mecca, in present-day Saudi Arabia, in 570. Islamic teaching explains that while Muhammad was meditating one day, the angel Gabriel appeared, instructing him to serve as a prophet. Muhammad started preaching and went on to become the leader of a religious community, his religious message becoming law. Islam's most sacred book, the Koran (or Quran), is believed to be the actual words of Allah as revealed by Gabriel over a period of many years. Muhammad's teachings and

Sufi shrine
Shown here is a *Sufi* shrine in Melilla, Morocco. Sufis are a small but influential Muslim sect in North Africa. Sufis are mystics who are opposed to materialism. They practice spiritual exercises involving dancing, chanting, and rhythmic movement.

Oldest mosque
The mosque of Ibn Tulun was built in 876–9 and is the oldest surviving mosque in Egypt.

sayings – the Hadith – were also collected and written down. They are considered a vital source for understanding Islam. The third most important Islamic text is the Sunna, a code of behavior based on Muhammad's example recorded in the Hadith.

Mosques

Mosques (Islamic houses of worship) follow a general pattern, based on the first prayer house built by Muhammad at Medina, in present-day Saudi Arabia. The basic plan of North African mosques is a large open space, generally protected by a roof. It contains two essential features. One is the mihrab, a semicircular niche in one wall that indicates the direction of Mecca, the holy city of Islam; Muslims must face toward Mecca when praying. Next to it stands the other feature, the minbar. This is a flight of steps leading up to a seat from which the preacher can address the congregation. Attached to most mosques is a minaret – a tall, slender tower with a platform at the top. From this platform a muezzin, or crier, calls the faithful to prayer. Many mosques are elaborately decorated, with carvings, inlay, and mosaic work.

Religious practices and duties

Devout Muslims must fulfil five duties: to profess the faith ("there is no god but Allah and Muhammad is His Prophet"); to pray five times a day; to try to make at least one pilgrimage (Hajj) to Mecca; to fast during Ramadan, the month that Allah called Muhammad to be His Prophet; and to regularly donate a proportion of their income or possessions to charity – the religious tax, or zakah.

The strictness of adherence to Islamic practices varies according to the traditions of particular societies and between individuals. For example, Islam calls on both male and female followers to dress modestly, but this is interpreted in widely differing ways, with only the strictest wearing all-enveloping veils.

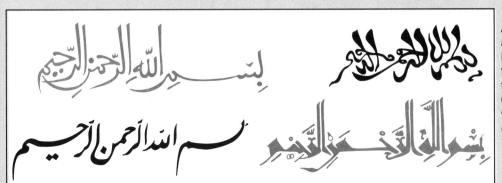

Calligraphic art
Arabic calligraphy is an art form in itself. Here, the phrase "In the name of Allah, the Merciful, the Compassionate" is written in four different styles.

Vanishing Jewish communities

Although there are only a few thousand Jews in North Africa today, until the foundation of Israel in 1948 and the rise of Arab nationalism in the 1950s and 1960s, the Jewish population numbered over 500,000. There were communities throughout North Africa, the majority of whom lived in the region's main towns and cities. Over the past few decades, the Jewish communities of Egypt, Libya, and Algeria have virtually ceased to exist, but a few small communities remain in Tunisia and Morocco.

History of settlement in North Africa

Between the sixth and third centuries BCE, *many Jews emigrated from Palestine to Egypt and the region of present-day Libya. Their settlement was encouraged by the Egyptians to populate and defend border regions. Communities were established elsewhere in North Africa, with Jewish traders reaching Morocco by the second century* BCE. *Following a failed Jewish revolt against Roman rule of Egypt in 115–17* CE, *the Egyptian Jewish community was destroyed and Jews were not to return for several centuries. Elsewhere, Jews participated in resistance to the Muslim Arab invasion of North Africa in the seventh century with, for example, Berber converts to Judaism achieving a number of victories in Algeria.*

A Jewish family from Fez
Dressed in traditional costume, this Jewish family lived in Fez, Morocco, in the 1920s. Fez is one of North Africa's great commercial centers and was developed in part by Jewish traders. During the tenth and eleventh centuries, the city became a center of Jewish learning, attracting great *rabbis,* poets, and scholars from Spain. In modern times, the community has been much reduced by migration to Casablanca and abroad.

African refuge
During the European Middle Ages, the increase of Christian intolerance toward Judaism led to a period of Jewish expulsion. Between 1492 and 1497, many Jews from Spain, Portugal, Sardinia, and Sicily settled in the towns and cities of North Africa.

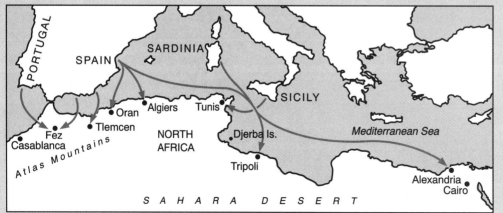

PORTUGAL
SPAIN
SARDINIA
SICILY
Oran
Algiers
Tunis
Tlemcen
Fez
Casablanca
NORTH AFRICA
Djerba Is.
Mediterranean Sea
Atlas Mountains
Tripoli
Alexandria
Cairo
S A H A R A   D E S E R T

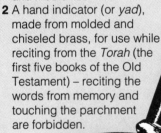

The Great Synagogue of Tunis
Built six centuries ago, this *synagogue* (Jewish house of worship) is in the Jewish quarter and is the oldest in Tunis. Following the exodus of most of Tunisia's Jews after 1948, Tunis and the small island of Djerba off the Tunisian coast have the only two remaining sizable Jewish communities left in Tunisia.

Metalwork
Most North African Jews were artisans who made high-quality goods. These examples are from nineteenth-century Morocco.
1 Mortar and pestle made from brass and used for making cosmetics and medicines.
2 A hand indicator (or *yad*), made from molded and chiseled brass, for use while reciting from the *Torah* (the first five books of the Old Testament) – reciting the words from memory and touching the parchment are forbidden.

By 711, Arabs had conquered all of North Africa, and Jewish immigrants from southwest Asia soon followed the Arabs into Africa. In Egypt, a Jewish presence was reestablished, and by the twelfth century Egypt's Jewish population numbered between twelve and twenty thousand. Although the Arabs often pressured Jews to convert to Islam, most Jewish communities resisted Islamicization. New arrivals from southwest Asia strengthened Jewish communities and kept them in touch with religious developments elsewhere.

In 1492, Jews who refused to convert to Catholicism were expelled from Spain and in 1496 from Portugal. Morocco and Algeria were important destinations for those expelled, but Spanish Jews also settled in towns and cities elsewhere in North Africa. The Spanish Jews maintained a separate existence from the local Arabic-speaking Jewish communities, preserving their language (Ladino – a medieval form of Spanish using the Hebrew script) and religious rituals until modern times.

Under Muslim rule, the treatment of Jews varied. Although under some rulers Jews were much respected, only in the thirteenth century was Judaism officially tolerated. Following the Ottoman (Turkish) takeover of Egypt in 1517 and the extension of its empire across North Africa, discrimination was often harsh. Although the Ottomans continued to encourage Spanish Jews to settle in North Africa, they were confined to ghettos and limited to practicing a few occupations. Nevertheless, the treatment of Jews in North Africa was generally no worse – and sometimes better – than that experienced by Jews in Europe at the time.

In the nineteenth century, much of North Africa came under European influence or control. This brought great changes to the position of the Jewish communities and opportunities for Jews to improve

An example of a typical girl's dress
This Jewish girl, from south of the Atlas Mountains in Morocco, is wearing the traditional, everyday clothing of the 1930s. She is wearing an *izar* (a long, striped garment, usually red or white) that hangs down to her feet and is worn over a colored blouse called a *derra*.

their economic status. Many Jews identified closely with French culture, and Algerian Jews were given automatic citizenship by the French, an act resented by the Muslims, who were not given this status. Jews from other parts of the Ottoman Empire, North Africa, Italy, and Eastern Europe migrated to Egypt — attracted by the tolerant environment — to escape persecution or for economic reasons.

Berber Jews

It is believed that some of the survivors of the Jewish revolt against the Romans (115–17), and Jews who fled later waves of persecution, found refuge among Berbers in western Libya and in the mountains and desert regions of Morocco and Algeria. Many of the Berbers with whom they settled converted to Judaism. Although most Berbers had adopted Islam by the twelfth century, small isolated groups of Jewish Berbers continued to live in the High Atlas Mountains on the edge of the Sahara until the early twentieth century.

Typical occupations

North African Jews generally lived in urban ghettos and were small-scale merchants or itinerant peddlers. Many were poor artisans, often acquiring their professional skills — in particular tailoring,

Exodus
In the twentieth century, the majority of Jewish people in North Africa have emigrated to France, Canada, or Israel. The figures on the map show the numbers of Jewish people who have left each country since the mid-twentieth century. Many had suffered from persecution and resentment from other North African people.

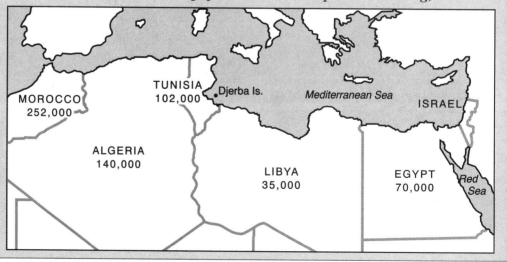

MOROCCO 252,000

TUNISIA 102,000 • Djerba Is.

ALGERIA 140,000

Mediterranean Sea

ISRAEL

LIBYA 35,000

EGYPT 70,000

Red Sea

leatherwork and metalwork, and filigreeing silver and gold jewelry – on a hereditary basis. In some areas, Jews dominated the wine trade, an activity prohibited to Muslims, cultivating vineyards and operating wine presses. This is the case even today on the Tunisian island of Djerba. A small Jewish elite also existed, basing their wealth on foreign trade and moneylending.

In the nineteenth century, occupational restrictions imposed on Jews were abolished, enabling them to become teachers, doctors, lawyers, and even politicians, and enabling merchants to expand into foreign trade and banking. Despite the position of Algerian Jews as French citizens and the newly acquired wealth and influence of some, it was not the Muslims who were most hostile to Jewish advances. It was the European settlers who most resented the competition from Jewish traders.

Departure from North Africa

The creation of Israel and the rise of Arab nationalism had a devastating effect on Jewish communities, which increasingly came under attack. During the Arab-Israeli war in 1948, hundreds of Egyptian Jews were arrested and their businesses seized. Bombings in Jewish areas of Cairo and Alexandria killed and injured hundreds of people. As a result, some 25,000 of Egypt's 70,000 Jews emigrated between 1948 and 1950. Most Jews, however, wanted to stay in Egypt, but nationalist measures threatened their schools, businesses, and jobs, leading to the emigration of virtually all Egyptian Jews within twenty years.

Elsewhere, Jews met with similar fates, most dramatically in Algeria, where in the early 1960s Jews found their loyalties tested in the violent war of independence against the French. Within a few years of Algeria's independence in 1962, almost the entire Jewish population of 140,000 had emigrated.

Only in Morocco and Tunisia do Jewish communities remain, though much reduced in number. From a Jewish population of 270,000 in 1948 there remain only about 18,000 Jews in Morocco, while in Tunisia the population fell from 105,000 to just 3,000. In Morocco, the majority live in Casablanca, though some remain in other ancient Jewish centers.

The Jews of North Africa are now widely scattered, living mainly in France, but also in Israel, Canada, and elsewhere. Wherever they settled, however, separate community institutions and synagogues were established, preserving in exile aspects of the North African Jewish tradition.

An example of a typical boy's dress This Jewish schoolboy is from one of the last Jewish communities of the southern Atlas Mountains in Morocco. He is wearing the traditional male costume of the 1920s and 1930s, including the *akhnif* (a long, beautifully embroidered cape).

Baggara

The Baggara (or Baqqara) of southwestern Sudan are descended from Bedouin Arabs and Black Africans with whom the Bedouin intermarried. There are over one million Baggara divided into more than twenty subgroups; some of the major subgroups are the Messiriya, Habbania, and Reizegat of Darfur province and the Humr of the Bahr al Arab region.

History

Bedouin Arabs are thought to have entered North Africa from southwest Asia sometime after or during the eleventh century. By the eighteenth century, the descendants of these Bedouin who became the Baggara were settled in present-day southern Sudan.

MAHDISTS Some Muslims believe that a holy person, the *Mahdi,* will one day come to earth as a savior and liberator. In 1881, a religious leader called Muhammad Ahmad announced that he was the Mahdi and in 1882 led a revolt against the British and Egyptian conquerors of Sudan. His armies won several spectacular victories and drew much of their support and troops from the Baggara. After his death in 1885, the Mahdi was succeeded by a Baggara man called Abdullah ibn

Baggara timeline

c. 1000s	Bedouin Arabs enter North Africa from Arabia
1500s	Baggara migrate into present-day eastern Sudan
1700s	Baggara settled in present-day southern Sudan
1821	Trade routes opened from north to south Sudan
1840s	Arab slave trade develops; Baggara active as traders
1881	Muhammad Ahmad declares himself "Mahdi"
1882	Anglo-Egyptian forces conquer Sudan
1882–1883	Mahdist revolution overthrows Anglo-Egyptian rulers
1885	Mahdists take Khartoum. Abdullah ibn Muhammad succeeds Mahdi as Khalifa
1898	Anglo-Egyptian force conquers Mahdist State; Khalifa killed
1955	First civil war between south and north Sudan begins
1956	Sudanese independence
1972	South granted regional autonomy; civil war ends
1983	Sudan adopts *Sharia* (Islamic holy) law against wishes of non-Muslim south; civil war erupts again
1985	Government begins training and arming Baggara militia
1988	Formation of Baggara Popular Defense Front (PDF)
1990s	PDF accused of "ethnic cleansing" of Nuba people as civil war continues

SAHEL

SUDAN

• Al Obeid

An-Nahud •

Nyala •

• Al Fula

Nuba Hills

White Nile

DARFUR PROVINCE

Bahr al Arab

Lol

Bahr al Ghazal

Sobat

Jur

Bahr al Jabal (Nile)

Jonglei Canal

S U D

• Waw

0	100	200 km

0	100 mi

Baggara man
Pictured in the early twentieth century, this spear-carrying Baggara man sitting astride his bull depicts a disappearing way of life. Although the Baggara rarely carry spears in modern Sudan, cattle are still of central importance. In fact, the name "Baggara" is derived from the Arabic word for cow – "bagar."

Muhammad, who was called the *Khalifa* (successor). Under the Khalifa, the Mahdist State expanded and the Sudanese were united. Although the Khalifa lead the Mahdist armies with great success, they were eventually defeated, and the Khalifa killed, by an Anglo-Egyptian force in 1898.

RECENT EVENTS In 1983, the Sudanese government adopted *Sharia* (Islamic holy) law against the wishes of the mainly non-Muslim south. Long-standing animosities between the north and south erupted in a civil war between government troops and southern-based rebels. Although living in the south, the Baggara have aligned themselves with their fellow Muslims in the north. This has meant that they are at war with many of their neighbors – in particular, the Nuba.

The Baggara began organizing themselves for operations against the Nuba as early as 1984. In 1985, rebels attacked a Baggara village in the Nuba Hills. The government responded by beginning its policy of supplying arms and military training to the Baggara

© DIAGRAM

Baggara woman
This Baggara woman is wearing necklaces and other items of jewelry made from gold and silver. Some Baggara women wear a lot of jewelry. Baggara women generally manage their own finances and often this jewelry is literally a woman's savings.

41

Headgear *(above)*
Many Baggara men shave their heads as a defense against insects and then wrap their heads in white cloth, as shown above.

Ceremonial camel
Elaborate ceremonial decorations – such as the one shown, which is made of leather set with cowrie shells – are used by some well-off Baggara women to adorn their camels.

groups. One branch of these local militias was organized into the Popular Defense Force (PDF) by the government in 1988. Since then, the Baggara militias have fought many battles against the rebels, often alongside government troops. They have also been accused of burning and looting Nuba villages and killing Nuba civilians. During the 1990s, the PDF has been heavily involved in the government's policy of "ethnic cleansing" against the Nuba people. Despite many cease-fires, the civil war continues today and many ordinary Baggara are caught between government troops, rebels, and their own militias.

Language

The Baggara speak a dialect of Arabic.

Ways of life

Most Baggara are cattle herders, and some men – only men own cattle – have herds several thousand strong. The land they live in is largely *savanna* (grasslands with a few trees and shrubs) and lies between the semidesert Sahel to the north and the seasonally swampy Sudd to the south. The Sahel does not always have enough rain to support cows, and the presence of disease-bearing *tsetse flies* and mosquitoes in the Sudd prevent cattle-rearing. So, during the summer rains, the Baggara and their herds move north to benefit from seasonal pastures. The Baggara temporarily settle and grow crops of sorghum and cotton, which is sold for cash. As the rainfall gets heavier, mosquitoes and tsetse flies flourish and the men move farther north with their herds, leaving the women to continue cultivating the crops. A few weeks later, the women and children join the men. When the northern grasslands become parched, the Baggara move back to harvest their crops. During the dry season, they move farther south – the mosquitoes and flies have now mostly died – to seek water and pastures.

Some men travel abroad for a year or two and work in various industries. The money earned is often used to pay their children's school fees or to buy more cattle.

Improvements in cattle-rearing and greater access to veterinary care have meant that the natural wastage of herds through disease has decreased. The Baggara have, therefore, been able to amass larger herds of cattle. Also, in order to control the Baggara better, the Sudanese government has adopted policies to encourage them to settle down – such as the boring of water holes and making school education compulsory for children. Larger herds, combined with more-settled lifestyles, have put a great strain on the fragile semidesert and savanna environments. Overgrazing of the land is fast becoming a severe problem. These changes have threatened the *seminomadic* lifestyle of the Baggara, which is ideally suited to an environment of scarce water resources and little vegetation.

Social structure

POLITICAL STRUCTURE Each group has a leader called a *nazir* – an Arabic word meaning "overseer." A large group may have two nazirs. The nazir acts as the official link with the Sudanese government. Every group also has several lesser officials called *omda*, who each look after a particular section. The omda are responsible for collecting taxes and settling disputes.

SOCIAL STRUCTURE The basic domestic unit is a woman and her young children, with an associated male such as the husband – who may have more than one wife, and therefore household of which he is a part. Married women control the domestic finances and earn significant amounts of money from the sale of milk to cheese factories and of butter and yogurt at markets.

MARRIAGE When a Baggara man marries, he gives his new wife's parents a gift of cattle, the *bridewealth*. By custom, his first wife is usually a cousin. A man can have several wives if he is rich enough to support them, but all wives should be treated equally.

Culture and religion

RELIGION The majority of Baggara are Muslims. Many Baggara men make the pilgrimage (*Hajj*) to Mecca, often staying for a few years to earn some money.

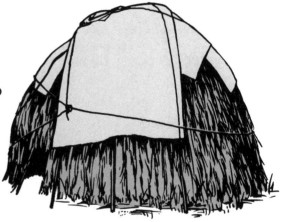

Traditional Baggara tent
The tents used by the Baggara have to be portable and easy to dismantle, so they are made from materials that are either readily available in the local area or are easy to carry. Sticks to make the basic framework can be cut at the campsite itself. Strips of bark and then mats, plastic sheeting, or cow hides are arranged to cover the sticks – these materials are usually carried from place to place. Traditional tents are beehive-shaped, cylindrical, or hemispherical, depending on which Baggara group they are made by. Some Baggara people give their tents conical thatched roofs.

© DIAGRAM

Foods and food taboos

Foods and diets vary greatly in North Africa. In the cities, particularly those of the Mediterranean coast, reasonably well-off people eat a mixed diet comparable in quality, though not necessarily in type, with diets of the West; poorer people tend to eat less well. In the desert and underdeveloped rural areas, people are largely dependent on what they can grow for themselves. In addition, there are many dietary restrictions imposed by religion or custom. The Muslim month of Ramadan is marked by great feasts held at the beginning and end of the month-long fast. During this fast, food and drinks can only be consumed out of daylight hours.

City foods

Generally, food along the North African coast is strongly influenced by Arab, European, and Turkish cultures – the last is a legacy of the Turkish Ottoman Empire, which once ruled much of North Africa. In the Maghreb (Algeria, Morocco, and Tunisia) the two most popular food and drink items in the cities are couscous and mint tea. Couscous is a steamed, coarse-ground grain such as semolina. It is normally eaten with a meat or vegetable stew.

Many people eat couscous almost every day and there are a great many variations on the basic recipe. It is a communal dish, so is usually served in large bowls from which everyone can help themselves. Mint tea, made with tea leaves and sprigs of fresh mint, is served hot and sweet in very small cups. People often drink this tea many times a day.

Tunisian cooks favor fish as a main stew ingredient – a wide variety of seafood is available along the northern coast. Vegetables eaten in North African cities include eggplant, broad beans, celery, cucumbers, leeks, lettuce, onions, spinach, sweet peppers, tomatoes, and zucchini. Fruit is varied and plentiful. The shops in the souks (marketplaces) in the old quarters of the cities abound with fruit, vegetables, and great mounds of ground spices. In Algeria and Tunisia, cayenne and chili are popular spices used in cooking.

Rice is a basic dish outside the Maghreb and bread is eaten everywhere. People usually make round, flat loaves of bread using a minimum of raising agent, or leaven. Most bread is made from wheatflour, but Tunisians like a bread made from semolina.

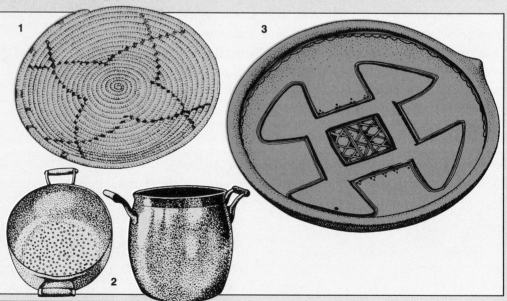

Couscous utensils

1 A large woven basket called a *tbeck,* used to contain couscous grains that have been sorted according to size.
2 A lidded pot called a *keskes* in which couscous is steamed.
3 An early twentieth-century, terra-cotta couscous dish from Algeria, which is large enough for many people to eat from.

Tea preparation
A desert nomad pouring mint tea. Typically, tea preparation involves adding boiling water to tea leaves, sprigs of mint, and sugar, pouring into glasses, and then pouring back into the pot before serving. This makes the tea cool enough and strong enough to drink.

Desert foods

The availability of food in the Sahara Desert depends on the activities of people. In the oases (fertile pockets of the desert), fresh vegetables and fruit are available. Oasis farmers grow barley, corn, millet, and wheat and make unleavened bread and pancakes from flour. Dates, from date palms, are used for food and as trade goods.

Nomadic peoples who travel with their herds in search of pasture and water have a spartan diet relying mainly on milk and milk products such as cheese and yogurt. On treks across the desert, nomads often eat one meal a day, but may have two when in camp. They make a gruel from grain blended with butter or sour milk. Meat tends to be reserved for special feasts, because the animals are more valuable as sources of milk or cash. Old and infirm camels are used as meat from time to time, and wild animals such as gazelles (small antelopes) and lizards are eaten. Camel meat and fish — when available — are frequently salted and sun-dried to be carried along as iron rations. Nomadic peoples drink tea or coffee when they can obtain them.

Foods of the plains and hills

People who live mainly by agriculture and herding — such as the Dinka and Baggara of Sudan — grow millet, barley, sorghum, and some vegetables for their own use. Pumpkins and melons are also grown. Corn, an American crop, is now grown by many people; sometimes it is ground and made into a porridge. Tamarinds (a type of evergreen tree) produce seed pods that can be pressed into cakes or made into a refreshing drink. These foods are supplemented by the meat of chickens, goats, and sometimes pigs. Fishing is also a major source of food for many coastal and riverine people.

Food taboos

There is a great variety of food taboos (prohibitions) in North Africa. Many Muslims do not eat pork or drink alcohol as these are forbidden under the Islamic code. In southern Sudan, however, non-Muslims raise pigs for food, and some Algerians make wine for export. Adult Tuareg of a group who live in the Ahaggar Mountains of southern Algeria will not eat chicken or chicken eggs under any circumstances. The reasons behind this taboo are not known.

© DIAGRAM

45

Beja

The Beja live in northeastern Sudan and northern Eritrea, between the Red Sea and the Nile River. There are half a dozen main Beja groups. The Hadendowa live along the Gash *watercourse* (a seasonally dry river) and are the most numerous group. Other groups include the Ababda, who live near the coast; the Amarar, who live around Port Sudan; and the Beni Amer and the Tigre, who live mostly in the south of northeastern Sudan and the north of Eritrea. Today, there are probably over 800,000 Beja.

History

The Beja have lived in the region where they are today for at least 5,000 years and are mentioned in ancient Greek, Egyptian, and Roman writings.

Language

Different Beja groups speak different languages. The Beni Amer and the Tigre speak Tigrinya, a Semitic language derived from an ancient Ethiopian language. Most Ababda speak Arabic. The rest of the Beja speak a language that is also called Beja (or To Bedawi).

Beja timeline

c. 3000–2000 BCE	Ancient Egyptians mine gold in northern Beja territories
100s ce	Axumite Kingdom emerges in Tigre lands: southern Beja adopt Tigrean class structure and language, Tigrinya
600s	Beja convert to Christianity. Decline of Axumite Kingdom
640	Arab conquest of North Africa begins: Islam introduced
c. 1150–1300s	The vast majority of Beja convert to Islam
1882	Mahdist revolution in Sudan begins; many Hadendowa become Mahdist warriors
1885	Battle at Tofrek between Anglo-Egyptian force and Mahdists. Anglo-Egyptian force supported by Bisharin and Amarar is defeated
1898	Britain and Egypt conquer Mahdist State
1955	First civil war between north and south Sudan begins
1956	Sudanese independence
1972	South granted regional autonomy; end of first Sudanese civil war
1978	Port Sudan: modernization and enlargement begins
1983	Sudan adopts *Sharia* (Islamic holy) law against wishes of the mainly non-Muslim south; civil war breaks out again
1990s	Despite many cease-fires, the Sudanese civil war continues
1993	Eritrea officially independent from Ethiopia

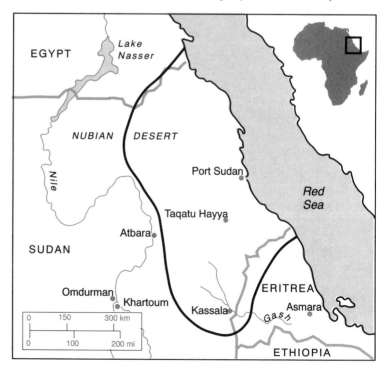

Ways of life

For many years, the Beja have lived by herding sheep and goats, with cattle in the south and camels in the north. One group, the Bisharin, are famous camel breeders. These animals provide them with milk, butter, and meat. The men tend the flocks and do the milking, while the women grow crops, mostly sorghum and cotton. Most Beja are *nomadic* (they travel with their herds in search of pasture and water). Some keep on the move all year round, while others move seasonally.

RECENT CHANGES As with other nomadic groups, the Sudanese government has encouraged the Beja to settle down. In the more fertile areas of the south, this has been achieved with success by some groups. Cotton and grain are the most common crops grown. The Hadendowa, in particular, have adopted sedentary cotton farming in large numbers. In fact, cotton cultivation along the Gash watercourse is largely controlled by Hadendowa farmers.

Other changes have been brought about by economic growth. The development of Port Sudan into a busy commercial centre has changed the lifestyles of many Beja. The Amarar, for example, previously lived in north Sudan but are now settled around Port Sudan and many work in its docks. Farther inland, other Amarar now graze cattle and sheep to sell in Port Sudan.

Social structure

Social organization differs from group to group. Some groups comprise one or more family units led by the most senior male. Others, such as the Tigre, have a distinct class system, with divisions between the nobility and ordinary citizens.

Culture and religion

RELIGION Under the influence of Christian Ethiopia, the Beja converted to Christianity about twelve centuries ago. However, after the seventh-century invasion of North Africa by the Arabs – who brought with them Islam – many converted to Islam. Since the fourteenth century, the majority of Beja have been Muslims.

Beja warrior (above)
Pictured in the early twentieth century, the look of this Amarar man recalls the reputation the Beja had for being great warriors.

Beja sword (left)
The design of this Beni Amer sword and scabbard is thought to have been influenced by swords that were used during the European crusades of the eleventh to thirteenth centuries.

© DIAGRAM

47

Music and dance in North Africa

Music and dance are an essential feature of celebrations in North Africa. In the cities, there are professional orchestras complete with singers and dancers, who hire themselves out for celebrations. A female singer is known in Morocco as a chikha. In Tunisia, the equivalent word is mashta. Most players are part-timers, because they find it difficult to make a living from music alone. The instruments they play include violins, lutes, mandolins, flutes, oboes, and drums. The violins are an import from across the Mediterranean Sea, but other instruments tend to be traditional North African ones. For example, the oboe equivalent in a North African orchestra is likely to be a shawm, which is an ancestor of the modern oboe. Many musicians play regional bowed instruments, such as the rabab, a folk fiddle descended from the medieval rebec. The rabab is more likely to be played by a street musician than in an orchestra though. Tunisian instruments include the mezonad, a form of bagpipe, much used by snake charmers.

One form of popular music in Morocco is called chaabi. Chaabi groups can be heard at festivals, in cafes and souks (markets), and in village squares. The music is a mix of Arab, Berber, and contemporary Western styles, and the lyrics tend to highlight political and social issues.

Berber music

Some groups of professional Berber musicians are called rwais. A rwai performance will include poetry and dance as well as music. A rwai group will have several singers; instruments include the rabab, lutes, and cymbals. Another type of Berber group is the imdyazn, usually made up of four musicians, including a poet as leader. Instruments include drums, rabab, and ghaita (a type of reed instrument).

Bandair and shawm players (above)
These Algerian musicians are shown playing a *bandair*, a tambourinelike instrument (left), and a type of reed instrument called a *shawm*.

Bagpipes (left)
These North African bagpipes each have a single mouth pipe and double chanters that produce the notes.

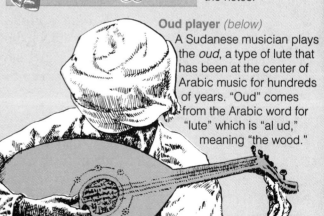

Oud player (below)
A Sudanese musician plays the *oud*, a type of lute that has been at the center of Arabic music for hundreds of years. "Oud" comes from the Arabic word for "lute" which is "al ud," meaning "the wood."

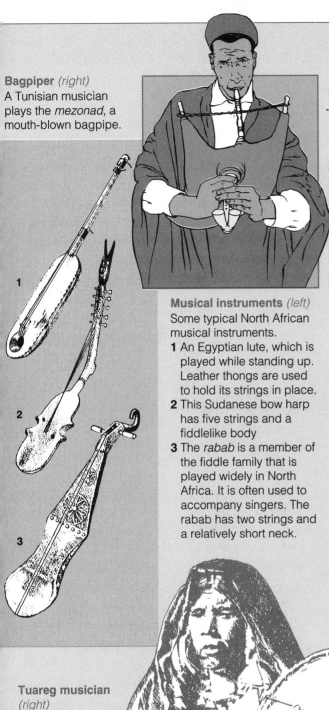

Bagpiper (right)
A Tunisian musician plays the *mezonad*, a mouth-blown bagpipe.

Musical instruments (left)
Some typical North African musical instruments.
1 An Egyptian lute, which is played while standing up. Leather thongs are used to hold its strings in place.
2 This Sudanese bow harp has five strings and a fiddlelike body
3 The *rabab* is a member of the fiddle family that is played widely in North Africa. It is often used to accompany singers. The rabab has two strings and a relatively short neck.

Tuareg musician (right)
This Tuareg woman is playing a drum. Among the Tuareg, it is mostly the women who are musicians.

Imdyazn usually play during the summer, traveling from village to village and often playing at the weekly markets.

In the High Atlas Mountains of Morocco, professional Berber musician-dancers are known as chleuh. *The leader of the group plays on a form of rabab with a single horsehair string. The accompaniment is provided by the gumbri, a small three-stringed lute, with the* naqqara, *a simple kettledrum, and the* bandair, *a large tambourine with snares, beating out the rhythm. The Tuareg and other* nomadic *people play instruments that are easily portable, such as pipes and drums. Berber singers tend to use Arabic, especially for ritual music, but some groups mainly use Berber languages.*

Arab music

The Arab conquerors of North Africa brought with them not only their religion and their language, but also much of their culture. Arab music covers a range of styles, from urban pop to Sudanese swing to the "belly-dance" rhythms. The instruments used are those found all over North Africa, especially those of the Maghreb *(Morocco, Algeria, Tunisia). What is different about Arab music is its structure. It uses up to twenty different modes – which compare with the modes or scales of medieval Europe – that are built up from twenty-four quarter-tone intervals; Western scales are based on eight-note sequences. One of the most popular forms is the* nuba, *a suite of several movements. In Egypt and Libya, the nuba has eight movements, played on lute, zither, violin, flute, and drum. In the Maghreb there is a different style of nuba, which developed in Spain during the "Moorish" (Arab and Berber) occupation of that country. Most musicians only remember a few of these nuba though.*

Music of Egypt

Music and dance have been a feature of Egyptian life for over 3,000 years. Tomb wall paintings show people playing flutes, clarinet- and oboe-like instruments, trumpets, harps, lyres, tambourines, castanets, and drums. The remains of harps, lyres, trumpets, flutes, and bells have been found in tombs.

Something of the old traditions survives in folk music. Various kinds of flutes, clarinets, oboes, and drums are common. The traditional instrument of the rural Egyptians is the arghul, *a type of double clarinet. Among the twentieth-century greats of Egyptian music are Muhammad Abd al Wahaab, a singer and composer who is credited with modernizing Arabic music, and Umm Kalthum, widely considered one of the greatest singers of the Arab world. Kalthum's legendary status has continued even after her death in 1975.*

Music of Sudan

Each of the various ethnic groups of Sudan has its own musical traditions. Most music is associated with religious festivals or social ceremonies and includes singing and dancing. Drums are a major feature, especially in southern Sudan, where a lot of music is based around five notes and is different from the Arabic rhythms of the north. The Baggara, on the other hand, do use Arabic scales, and their music reflects the rhythms of cattle herding.

A common melody instrument is the lyre, which goes under a number of different names, such as tambour *among the Nubians and* brimbiri *among the Nuba; it is also sometimes called a* kissar. *Most Sudanese lyres have metal strings. Harps and one-stringed fiddles of the rabab type are also used. Sudanese people play a variety of wind instruments, including flutes, trumpets, and horns.*

Lyrics

In some North African music, the voice is used for chanting and other wordless sounds rather than to sing lyrics. But many North Africans use lyrics as a powerful medium for conveying a political stance or other message. In Sudan, for instance, lyrics have been used both by the Dinka — to praise the leader of the Sudanese People's Liberation Army (SPLA), Colonel John Garang — and by followers of the former military dictator Colonel Gaafar Muhammad Nimeri to ignite nationalistic feelings, in an attempt to unite his war-torn country. 1960s Nubian lyrics mourn the loss of their homeland, which was flooded by the building of the Aswan High Dam. In Algeria, the lyrics of the young, antiestablishment rai *singers usually express their frustration with both the government and the growing radical Islamic fundamentalist movement.*

"King of Rai"
Cheb Khaled is one of the most popular rai singers and is now a star in Europe and India as well as his native Algeria.

Whirling dervishes (left)

Dervishes are *Sufi* Muslims, who follow a special form of Islamic mysticism. Dervishes are dedicated to a life of poverty and chastity. Sufis and dervishes are found throughout North Africa. Their devotional rituals tend to send the dervishes into a trance. In this state, they break into wild dances in which they spin around and around.

Mulid band (right)

These band members are performing at a *mulid,* a huge Sufi festival. The Sufis, Islamic mystics, differ from other Muslims in their use of music as a spiritual influence.

Rai: a modern twist to an old art

Hugely popular today in Algeria and Morocco, the music known as rai has produced many international stars. Rai has roots in the music of Algerian rural musicians from several centuries ago, called cheikhs, *but in the early twentieth century their mostly poetic and nonpolitical songs were dropped by a new generation of rebellious women* cheikhas. *By the 1970s, rai had developed into a form of protest music for disaffected Algerian youth. The musicians, many of whom prefix their name with Cheb or Chaba, combine traditional instruments such as the* darabouka (*a clay drum*) *with synthesizers, bass guitars, and drum machines to create danceable rhythms, which are played in clubs and discos.*

Dancing

Music is often accompanied by dancing. In some groups men and women dance together, in others separately. Traditional dance styles include the vertical springing of the Dinka, the loping stomp of some Saharan nomads, and the whirling of some Muslims. At Islamic family celebrations and other gatherings, the women and men are separated. This gives the women more freedom to express themselves through dance, which can be quite erotic. The Koran does not forbid either music or dancing, but strict Muslims make distinctions between what they regard as moral and immoral performances.

Among some of the Tekna peoples of southern Morocco, the women dance on their knees. This is because they live (and dance) in low tents, where there is not enough headroom to stand upright. Rhythm for the dance is provided by a large cooking pot, the guedra, *which has an animal skin stretched over it to turn it into a drum. Nomadic peoples like the Tekna cannot afford to carry large numbers of items, so the pot does double duty.*

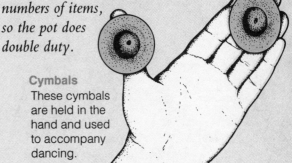

Cymbals
These cymbals are held in the hand and used to accompany dancing.

Berbers

T here are about fifteen million Berbers spread out over North Africa from Egypt to Morocco and south to the Sahel – the semidesert strip south of the Sahara Desert. The majority – about seven million – live in the Atlas Mountains of Morocco and Algeria. Others live in the *oases* (fertile pockets) that dot the Sahara. There are many different Berber groups: the Irifiyen of northeast Morocco; the Imazighen of central and southeast Morocco; and the Iqbailiyen of Algeria are just a few. The name "Berber" was given to them by the ancient Greeks. "Imazighen" is sometimes used to refer to all Berbers, as well as the Imazighen proper.

History

The Berbers are the earliest known inhabitants of North Africa and they were settled along the Mediterranean coast by 3000 BCE. By about 250 BCE, they had set up three kingdoms in what is now northern Morocco, Algeria, and Tunisia. At times, the Berbers were in conflict with their neighbors, the city-state of Carthage –

Berber timeline

3000 BCE	Berbers settled on North African coast
814	Carthage city-state founded
c. 250	Berbers establish Mauretania and two Numidian kingdoms
203	Berber kingdoms unified
201–148	Reign of King Masinissa over Numidia
201–46	Numidia encroaches on Carthaginian territory
c. 85–46	Reign of King Juba I over Numidia
46	Roman-ruled Carthage divides Numidia
640 CE	Arab invasion of North Africa begins; Islam introduced
711	Arabs control North Africa
1054	Almoravid dynasty founded
1069	Almoravid Empire covers northwestern North Africa
1086	Almoravids invade Spain
1147	Almohad dynasty founded
1150	Almohads take over Almoravid Empire
1269	End of Almohad Empire
1860s	French rule begins in northwest Africa
1920s	Abd al Krim leads wars against colonial powers
1956	Moroccan independence
1962	Algerian independence
1990	50,000 Berbers demonstrate in Algeria after Berber is outlawed
1992	Military coup in Algeria
1994	Berber officially accepted in Algeria and Morocco
1995	Multiparty elections in Algeria

near present-day Tunis – or the Romans who colonized parts of the coast. The Romans made an alliance with the Berber king, Masinissa, who ruled over a large area of North Africa called Numidia. He forced many Berbers to settle on the land as farmers and built up a strong kingdom, which broke up after his death. Another Numidian ruler, Juba I, created a Berber kingdom but was deposed by the Roman general Julius Caesar in 46 BCE.

ALMORAVIDS AND ALMOHADS The modern history of the Berbers, and the history traced by the Berbers themselves, begins with their conversion to Islam by the Arabs, who began to move into North Africa in 640 CE. Over the years, Arab invasions forced many Berbers out of the coastal regions and into the mountains and desert. Others were absorbed into the Arab population.

In 1054, a confederation of Muslim Berber groups formed a new and powerful dynasty in the west, in what is now southern Morocco and Western Sahara. They were known as the Almoravids. The whole of Morocco was under Almoravid rule by 1069. In 1086, they invaded Spain and had conquered much of its south by 1106. In 1147, another Berber confederation formed – the Almohads – and by 1150 the Almohads had taken over the whole Almoravid Empire, including their conquests in Spain. The Almohad Empire later collapsed, and they lost their last possessions in 1269. In Spain, the Almoravids and Almohads were known as "Moors" (not to be confused with the present-day Moors of Mauritania).

COLONIALISM All of North Africa was under at least nominal colonial rule by 1914. Resistance to European rule was strongest in Berber-speaking areas. The Berber leader Abd al Krim lead a war against the French in 1921 and against the Spanish and French from 1925 to 1926. North Africa was free from colonial rule by the 1960s.

Language

The Berber language, also called Berber, has over twenty different dialects. Berber is related to Ancient Egyptian but uses the Arabic script. Many Berbers also speak Arabic as well as French or Spanish. Although widely spoken, Berber is not an official language in any North

Lucky hand
The symbol of the hand is frequently used in jewelry worn by Berber women. It represents Islam's five fundamental principles, so it is called *khamsa* – the Arabic for "five." The khamsa is thought to protect against the "evil eye." The pendants shown here are worn on a chain; one has miniature stylized hands extending from the sides.

Mud castles
Mud-and-straw castlelike homes, such as the one shown here, can be found in Berber communities in the Atlas Mountains. They are not typical dwellings but would be lived in by the wealthy, by holy men, or by landowners.

© DIAGRAM

Facial tattoo
This Berber woman has tattoos on her face. Tattoos are traditionally used to identify which Berber group the wearer belongs to. The designs are often based on an ancient Libyan script. The jewelry that she is wearing is also very traditional and distinctively Berber. It incorporates coins, amber, silver, glass, and cloth.

African country. This reflects the fact that Berbers are often treated as second-class citizens by the dominant Arabs. In Algeria in 1990, for example, Arabic was made the sole official language and Berber was outlawed. Thousands demonstrated to demand that Berber be taught in schools. Both Morocco and Algeria finally gave Berber official recognition as a second language in 1994.

Ways of life

Although lifestyle varies from one Berber group to another and some Berbers live in cities, the vast majority are farmers. Vineyards and olive trees clothe the mountain slopes where many Berbers live. Staple crops include wheat, barley, and vegetables – turnips are commonly grown in the higher mountains. Apples and potatoes have become major cash crops since the 1980s. The Berbers raise a variety of animals such as cattle, sheep, goats, horses, and camels. Many Berbers rely on their animals for their livelihood and move with their herds according to the season to find the best pastures. Although *nomadic* in this sense, they still maintain permanent settlements where crops are grown. In farming communities, women tend to carry out domestic work while men farm and build houses. Exceptions to this include harvesting, collecting newly-cut grain, and whitewashing houses – tasks often done by women.

Since independence, many Moroccans and Algerians – including Berbers – have migrated to Europe, in particular France, where they work in various industries.

Mountain village
This Berber village rests in a valley of the High Atlas Mountains of central Morocco.

Social structure

POLITICAL STRUCTURE Berbers in the coastal regions are largely absorbed into the predominantly Arab culture and politics of the countries in which they live. In the more remote mountain and desert regions, however, traditional systems persist to a certain extent. Villages still have regular meetings of adult men, which in the past would decide questions of law and government. Nowadays, they usually deliberate on local issues.

SOCIAL STRUCTURE Southern Berber groups still maintain their precolonial social divisions. The top level comprises people who claim descent from the Prophet Muhammad. A middle level comprises the so-called "white Berbers" and the lower level of settled oasis cultivators are commonly known as *haratin*. In the past, the haratin – who are usually Black Africans – existed in a client relationship with a specific Berber group and would provide them with provisions when needed. Today, these social divisions are turning into a class system based largely on wealth and prosperity.

Berber women are generally more independent than Arab women. Many trade at the markets and manage their own finances.

MARRIAGE Women arrange marriages and wedding ceremonies. Berber girls tend to marry at the age of fifteen or sixteen. Some of these arranged marriages do not work out, however. If they break up in the first two weeks, the couple can divorce simply and are then free to seek partners of their own choosing.

Culture and religion

RELIGION The majority of Berbers follow Islam, which was introduced by Arab invaders in the seventh century. The Berbers themselves then became active in spreading Islam throughout the rest of northwestern Africa.

ART The only arts practiced that produce works which are recognizably Berber are carried out by women. Irifiyen female artisans are famous for their pottery decorating, for example, while the women of many groups in Morocco weave distinctive rugs.

Rug designs
This rug is typical of those made by the Zemmour, a Berber group in the Middle Atlas Mountains of northwest Morocco. It uses geometric shapes in several colors on a red background. Different groups use particular designs, techniques, and colors for their rugs. Women weave the rugs using sheep's or goats' wool, dyed with natural pigments.

© DIAGRAM

Rock art of the Sahara

The Sahara was not always a desert; 10,000 years ago it was a place of rivers and grassy plains. The people who lived there left records of their life in the Sahara from about 6000 to 100 BCE. These records are a series of paintings on the red sandstone rocks of Tassili-n-Ajjer, southeastern Algeria. Tassili-n-Ajjer is a bleak plateau scored with deep canyons and gorges. Its highest point is 7,400 ft (2,250 m) above sea level. The plateau is baking hot by day and bitterly cold at night. Tassili-n-Ajjer means "plateau of the rivers," and from the paintings it is obvious that there was once plenty of water around. The remains of a fossil forest show that its slopes were once wooded, but today it is hard to imagine elephants, giraffes, and other animals roaming the area. Several of the paintings are of hippopotamuses and archeologists have found bones of hippos in a dry riverbed south of Tassili-n-Ajjer. Other rock paintings in North Africa show crocodiles and men hunting from boats in areas that are now waterless.

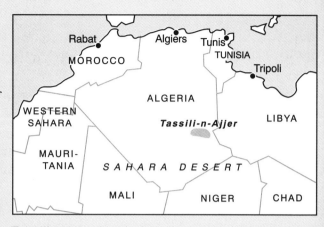

Tassili-n-Ajjer *(right and above)*
Tassili-n-Ajjer is a block of sandstone that has been carved by the erosive powers of water and wind into a maze of weird, pillarlike columns of rock separated by deep, dry gullies. The rock paintings are mostly found at the feet of these columns. The site lies at the heart of the Sahara Desert in the south of Algeria close to its border with Libya. Some of the ancient trans-Saharan trade routes once passed through this area.

Pastoralists *(below)*
From about 5000 to 1200 BCE the inhabitants of Tassili-n-Ajjer were *pastoral* people who herded cattle and other animals. The rock paintings from this time show herds of cattle and flocks of sheep and goats.

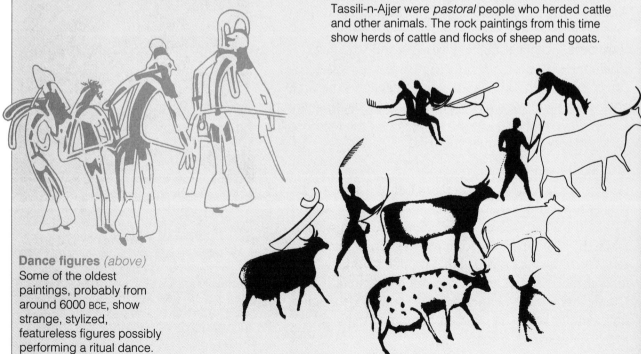

Dance figures *(above)*
Some of the oldest paintings, probably from around 6000 BCE, show strange, stylized, featureless figures possibly performing a ritual dance.

The earliest pictures show human figures wearing flared leggings and performing some kind of dance. These paintings probably date from 8,000 years ago. A thousand years later, artists were painting cattle, wild sheep, giraffes, and other animals. Giant buffaloes, which are now extinct, are often featured. Later paintings show horse-drawn chariots; camels begin to appear from around 100 BCE. Many of the paintings are on top of earlier ones. In places, there are as many as a dozen layers. This overpainting suggests that the artists regarded certain sites as sacred and that to make a new painting on one was a way of placating the gods.

The ancient artists of Tassili-n-Ajjer used a few bright colors — mostly yellow, red, and brown. They obtained these colors from ocher (a reddish-brown or yellow clay).

Hippo hunt *(left below)*
Hunting was a way of life for the people of the Sahara. It is thought that this painting shows a hippopotamus hunt, with the hunter in a canoe. This is further evidence that lakes and rivers once covered the Sahara.

Chariots *(below)*
This chariot painting is probably from around 1200 BCE, when invasions from the north brought chariots and warriors and led to the end of the long pastoral period in Tassili-n-Ajjer. The pastoralists were probably driven southward.

The lost colony of Carthage

According to legend, Dido, queen of the Phoenician city of Tyre, founded Carthage. She fled to North Africa with a small band of warriors after her brother murdered her husband. Dido asked the Berber inhabitants of the region for a plot of land on which to build a city; she was offered as much as could be surrounded by a bull's hide. She ordered the hide to be cut into thin strips, which laid end to end surrounded a large block of land.

Phoenicia was an ancient region of city-states in the coastal regions of present-day Syria and Lebanon. For hundreds of years, the trading ships of the Phoenicians dominated the waters of the Mediterranean Sea. In the course of trade they founded a number of colonies, the greatest of which was Carthage, founded in 814 BCE. Carthage stood on a promontory on the shores of the Gulf of Tunis, close to the modern city of Tunis. The sea defended Carthage on three sides. On the landward side, the Carthaginians built a huge wall, 30 ft (9 m) thick and more than 50 ft (15 m) high. Quarters for thousands of soldiers, horses, and 300 elephants were built nearby. Carthage replaced an older Phoenician settlement called Utica, which was about 15 miles (24 km) to the northwest. Carthage was probably independent from about 600 BCE.

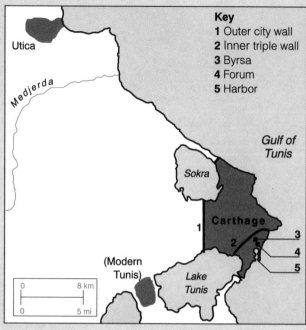

Key
1 Outer city wall
2 Inner triple wall
3 Byrsa
4 Forum
5 Harbor

Carthage had two excellent harbors and a large fleet of vessels. The oblong outer harbor was for merchant shipping. A narrow channel led to the circular inner harbor, which had berths for 220 warships. Trade with sub-Saharan Africa and across the Mediterranean Sea were the bases of Carthage's wealth and power. Dates and animal skins from the Sahara; ivory, slaves, and gold from West Africa; grain and copper from Sardinia; silver from Spain; tin from Britain; and grains, wine, glassware, and textiles from Carthage itself were traded.

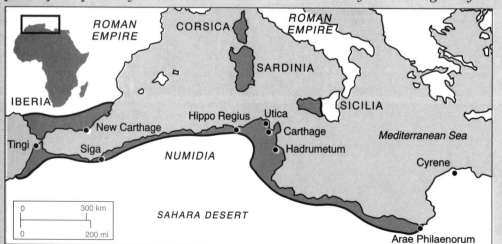

Hannibal's empire
Thanks to the military skills of the great Carthaginian general Hannibal (who lived 247–183 BCE), Carthage came to control most of the North African coast, parts of Spain and Sicily, and Corsica and Sardinia. It was their island possesions that brought Carthage into conflict with the Romans and led to the three Punic Wars.

Carthage, the site as it was *(left)*
At its height, Carthage covered the whole peninsula. An inner triple wall protected the main city areas, and an outer wall, most of the peninsula. The central Byrsa was a citadel (fortified stronghold).

Coinage
An African elephant appears on this Carthaginian coin. Carthage did not have its own curreny until c. 400 BCE. The Carthaginians managed to tame elephants and Hannibal used them in the invasion of Italy during the Second Punic War (218–201 BCE).

Statues
These terra-cotta heads show typical Carthiginian styles of dress. The man has a long beard but no mustache and the woman wears a long headdress. Both women and men often wore nose rings, as these heads show.

Daily life

People lived in houses with many floors that stood on very narrow streets; whole families often slept in just one room. At ground level were open-fronted shops. Sanitation was basic and the city suffered from repeated epidemics. Wealthy Carthaginians lived on estates outside the city, surrounded by orchards, farms, and Berber villages.

Carthaginian farmers concentrated on the intensive cultivation of almonds, figs, grapes, olives, pears, and pomegranates. Berber farmers supplied staple foods such as cereals and vegetables. Cattle, goats, horses, poultry, bees, and sheep were kept. Transportation was provided by mules and donkeys.

Carthaginian men wore long gowns with sleeves, and turbans or conical caps. Their hair was cut short and they had long pointed beards. Women wore long gowns and veils over their heads. Both men and women wore jewelry, including nose rings, and often used perfume. Carthaginian craftsmen and artists were greatly influenced by Greece in their work. Typically, though, Carthaginian statues had heavier, more robust forms than the finer Greek ones. Many artefacts and statues were imported from Greece or made by resident Greek artists. Carthage had an extensive library, most of which was destroyed by the invading Romans – except for an encyclopedia of farming techniques.

Carthaginian religion

The Carthaginians worshipped Phoenician deities – the Sun god Baal-Moloch and the Moon goddess Astarte. They renamed them Baal-Haman and Tanit-Pene-Baal, meaning "Tanit the Face of Baal." Priests served Baal-Haman and priestesses served Tanit. The Carthaginians mostly buried their dead and practiced embalming – archeologists have found many preserved bodies. Like the Egyptians, the Carthaginians made and buried grave goods for the afterlife. Most of these were terra-cotta models.

Decline of Carthage

For a long time, the local Berbers of Numidia were friendly to the Carthaginians, but eventually they turned against them under the leadership of King Masinissa (reigned 201–148 BCE). This conflict – when combined with a series of wars against the Romans, (the three Punic Wars, 264–146 BCE) – wore out the strength of Carthage. In 146 BCE, the Roman general Scipio Aemilianus captured the city and destroyed it. The Romans later built a new city of Carthage, but on a different site.

Copts

T here are roughly 6,000,000 Copts, who comprise the Christian minority in the predominantly Muslim country of Egypt.

History

Copts are the descendants of Egyptians who kept their Christian faith despite many periods of persecution under the Romans and the influence of Islam after the Arab invasion. The *Coptic* historical period began around the late 200s when a Copt, Saint Anthony of Egypt, founded the early Christian monastic movement. By 642, Muslim Arabs had conquered Egypt, ending the Coptic Period.

RECENT EVENTS The British colonizers of Egypt fostered divisions between Muslims and Christians. Over the years, these divisions have increased to outright persecution and physical attacks, and many Copts have emigrated to Canada, Australia, or the United States.

Language

The Coptic language is a version of Ancient Egyptian enriched with Greek words. It is written in a script

Copts timeline

c. 40	Christianity established
c. 60	Saint Mark visits Egypt
100s	Coptic language emerges
200s	Roman persecution of Copts
c. 250– 356	Life of Saint Anthony of Egypt (or Memphis or Thebes)
313	Edict of Milan legalizes Christianity in Roman Empire
392	Christianity becomes official religion of Roman Empire
450s	Byzantine persecution of Copts
451	Coptic Church established
642	Arabs conquer Egypt
725– 830	Riots against Islamic taxes on non-Muslims
969	Fatimid rule begins
1200s	Coptic language almost extinct
1250	Mamluk rule over Egypt begins
1517	Ottoman conquest of Egypt
1856	Hamayouni Decree attempts to achieve equality between Muslims and Copts in Egypt
1882	British colonize Egypt
1920s	Many Copts support the nationalist movement
1922	Egypt independent as a monarchy
1934	Laws introduced to hamper the building of churches
1952	Monarchy overthrown
1961	Nationalization begins
1970s	Coptic, Roman Catholic, and Eastern Orthodox churches consider reunion
1981– 1985	Coptic Pope under house arrest; he is accused of trying to be a political leader
1990s	Increasing attacks on Copts by radical Islamic fundamentalists

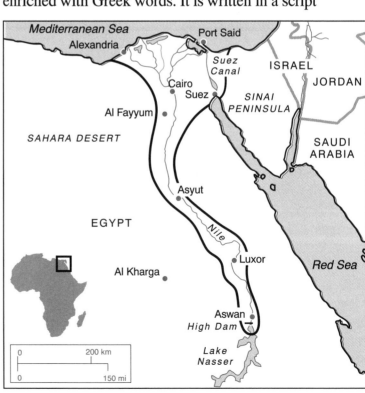

derived from the Greek alphabet. Coptic was in fact the last form of Ancient Egyptian to be used. After the Arab conquest of Egypt, the Coptic language gradually gave way to Arabic. By the 1300s, Coptic survived only in the liturgy (services) of the Coptic (Christian) Church. Today, Arabic is used for parts of the Coptic services.

Ways of life

The majority of Copts are farmers, as are their Muslim counterparts. In the past, although Copts were largely excluded from positions of power, they dominated the civil service and were frequently profitable business people. After the monarchy was overthrown in 1952, however, many of their jobs were abolished and much of their property nationalized. Considering that they form a small minority in Egypt, Copts are well represented in the professions, such as law, journalism, and medicine.

Culture and religion

RELIGION Most Copts are members of the Coptic Church, but a minority belong to other churches. Tradition states that Saint Mark brought Christianty to Egypt in c. 60, but Christian communities probably already existed in Egypt by this date. In 451, the Christian Church attempted to standardize its doctrine. The Council of Chalcedon was arranged to carry this out. Coptic Christianity differs from other forms in that it asserts the unity of both the human and the divine in the nature of Christ. This is referred to as the *Monophysite doctrine*. At the Council of Chalcedon, the church leaders from Constantinople and Rome condemned the Monophysite doctrine and declared that Christ had two separate natures. In response, the Copts established an independent church. The Coptic Period can therefore alternatively be dated from 451.

ART The early Copts included many fine artists and some of their paintings, sculptures, and textiles have survived. Most of them are on religious themes. Even after the Arab invasion of Egypt, Coptic artists continued to produce carvings, book bindings, and beautifully decorated manuscripts. Muslims often employed Coptic artists to decorate their buildings. In modern Egypt, Coptic art and culture is largely ignored by school curriculums.

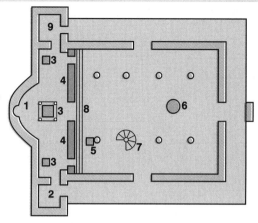

Plan of a Coptic church (*above*)
As with most churches, Coptic churches are built on an east-west axis. The nave (central part) is separated from the side aisles by columns. The south aisle is usually reserved for women. A screen called a *haikal* separates the sanctuary from the choir. The sanctuary is raised above the level of the choir.

Key
1 Clergy's seating area
2 Sacristy
3 Altar
4 Haikal
5 Episcopal throne
6 Water tank
7 Pulpit with spiral stairway
8 Steps
9 Baptistery

Crux ansata
This Coptic Period limestone panel, from the seventh or eighth century, was probably used as a wall decoration or tombstone. The carved cross is called a *crux ansata*. These crosses began to be used from the fifth century onward. The shape is based on the Ancient Egyptian *hieroglyph* (picture symbol) for "life" – the *ankh*.

© DIAGRAM

Ancient Egyptian society

Egypt has one of the world's oldest civilizations and has been in existence since c. 4500 BCE. The dynastic Egypt of the pharaohs (kings) emerged in c. 3100 BCE. At its greatest extent (in the 1400s BCE), the Kingdom of Egypt reached as far as present-day Syria. For one hundred years from c. 1670 BCE, Egypt was ruled by "Hyksos" – literally "foreigners." After the end of the Twentieth Dynasty in c. 1070 BCE, a period of decline set in. Various nations invaded Egypt, which then fell under their control: Nubians (Sudanese) from the 700s; Assyrians from 671; Persians from 525; and Macedonians (Greeks) under Alexander the Great from 332. After the death of Alexander, one of his generals, Ptolemy, claimed Egypt. His successors were known as the Ptolemies. They ruled Egypt until 30 BCE when it became part of the Roman Empire. Arabs from southwest Asia conquered Egypt in 642 CE and converted most of its people to Islam. Since this time, Egypt has been dominated by the language and culture of the Arabs.

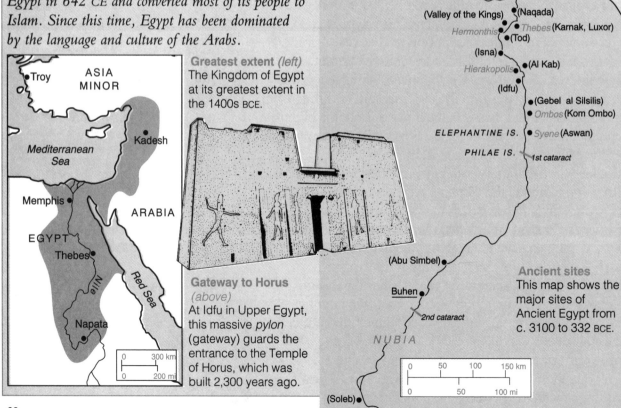

Akhetaton	Ancient Egyptian name
Memphis	Greco-Roman name
(Sakkara)	Modern name
LOWER EGYPT	Regional division (at times independent kingdoms)

Greatest extent (left)
The Kingdom of Egypt at its greatest extent in the 1400s BCE.

Gateway to Horus (above)
At Idfu in Upper Egypt, this massive *pylon* (gateway) guards the entrance to the Temple of Horus, which was built 2,300 years ago.

Ancient sites
This map shows the major sites of Ancient Egypt from c. 3100 to 332 BCE.

The gift of the Nile

Egyptian civilization arose in, and continues to be based around, the Nile Valley. Every year, beginning around July, the river flooded. When the floods retreated, around September, they left a deposit of rich, black, fertile soil along each bank about 6 miles (10 km) wide. Here, the Ancient Egyptians grew their crops. In an otherwise arid environment, the Nile provided water for irrigation as well as fertile soil. In ancient times, the river was the main transport route and most of Ancient Egypt's population lived in the Nile Valley. For these reasons, Ancient Egypt has been described as "the gift of the Nile."

Daily life in Ancient Egypt

Egyptian society had three main classes: upper, middle, and lower. The upper class comprised the royal family, religious and government officials, army officers, doctors, and wealthy landowners. Merchants, artisans, and manufacturers made up the middle class. There were many skilled workers such as architects, engineers, teachers, accountants, stonemasons, and carpenters. The majority of people, however, were of the lower class — laborers who mostly worked on farms owned by the upper classes. The main crops grown were wheat and barley, which were often given as wages to the workers. Other crops included vegetables and fruit. Bread made from wheat was the staple food and beer made from barley the main drink. Flax was grown to make linen. Farmlands were irrigated with water taken from canals. Antelopes, cattle, goats, sheep, donkeys, and pigs were raised. Egyptians also kept dogs and cats, and at one time hyenas.

The Ancient Egyptians made many long-lasting contributions to worldwide civilization. They established the first national government, built many great cities, and devised a 365-day calendar.

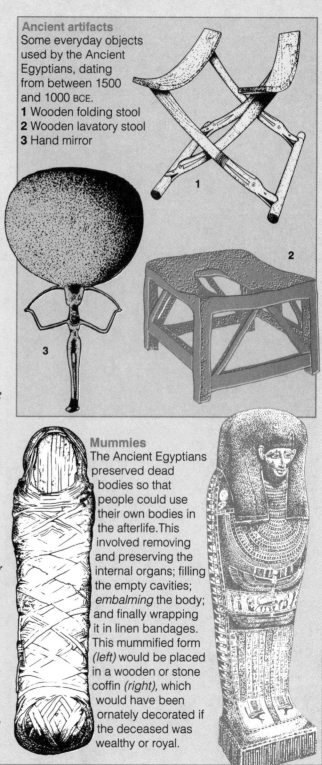

Ancient artifacts
Some everyday objects used by the Ancient Egyptians, dating from between 1500 and 1000 BCE.
1 Wooden folding stool
2 Wooden lavatory stool
3 Hand mirror

Mummies
The Ancient Egyptians preserved dead bodies so that people could use their own bodies in the afterlife. This involved removing and preserving the internal organs; filling the empty cavities; *embalming* the body; and finally wrapping it in linen bandages. This mummified form *(left)* would be placed in a wooden or stone coffin *(right)*, which would have been ornately decorated if the deceased was wealthy or royal.

Ancient Egyptian religion

Ancient Egyptians believed in an afterlife and many gods and goddesses who ruled over different aspects of the world. The most important of these was the Sun god Re, who could grant good harvests, and the creator-god Ptah. The fertiltiy goddess Isis, wife and sister of Osiris (judge of the dead), was the mother of Horus, the lord of Heaven. The pharaohs were believed to be incarnations of Horus. Every city and town also had its own particular god or goddess. The people of Thebes, for instance, worshipped a Sun god called Amon. Over time, Amon became identified with Re and was known as Amon–Re.

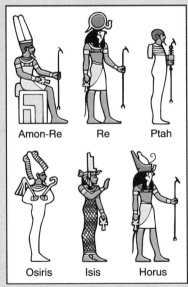

Amon-Re   Re   Ptah

Osiris   Isis   Horus

Egyptian deities
These pictures of Ancient Egyptian deities have been executed in a typically stylized fashion. Some are portrayed as having human bodies with animal heads, which reflect the different natures of the deities and helped make identification easier.

Tutankhamen
Few Ancient Egyptian tombs survived untouched until the twentieth century. One that did was that of an unimportant pharaoh, the boy-king Tutankhamen, who died more than 3,300 years ago at the age of eighteen. The tomb, which is in the Valley of the Kings, has four rooms that contained more than 5,000 objects. Many objects were made of gold, such as this beautifully engraved mask, which covered the face of the dead king's *mummy*.

Cattle inspection
This ancient wall painting from a tomb shows a herder having his cattle counted and recorded.

Hieroglyphic writing

Ancient Egyptians used picture symbols called hieroglyphs to represent ideas and sounds. They were used from c. 3000 BCE until after 300 CE when a new alphabet was introduced. Over 700 symbols were used.

a or o	ch	d
arm	placenta	hand
mt	**n**	**r**
vulture	water	mouth
s	**t**	**sh**
folded linen	loaf	pool

Hieroglyphs were most often used for religious and royal inscriptions in stone. Usually, trained scribes carved or wrote using hieroglyphs. As the demand for written records and communications grew, there was a need to simplify the process. The invention of paper made from papyrus (reedlike plants), pens made from sharpened reeds, and ink made by mixing soot and water, enabled writing to become more commonplace. Simplified forms of hieroglyphs developed called hieratic *and* demotic, *which were suitable for writing quickly on papyrus.*

The Age of Pyramids

The Egyptian pyramids are tombs that were built for royals and nobles. They are the oldest and largest stone structures in the world. Imhotep, a great architect, built the first – the Step Pyramid – for King Zoser in c. 2650 BCE. *The following 500 years are known as the "Age of Pyramids" because many of the most magnificent pyramids were built during this time. Royalty and nobles spent fortunes building these elaborate tombs, which were stocked with everything a person could wish for in the afterlife. Many skilled craftsmen were employed to decorate and furnish the tombs. As thieves robbed many of the pyramids in ancient times, tombs were increasingly built in secret underground locations, such as the Valley of the Kings near Thebes, and without a pyramid to attract looters.*

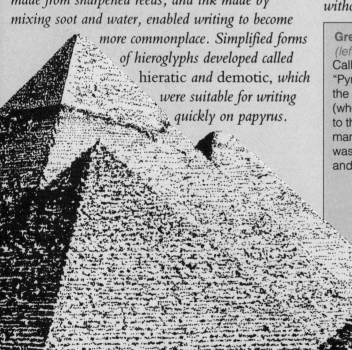

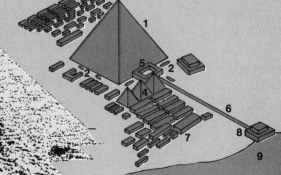

Great Pyramid of Khufu
(left and below)
Called by the Egyptians the "Pyramid that is the Sunset," the Great Pyramid of Khufu (who was known as Cheops to the Greeks) is only one of many at the site of Giza. It was begun in c. 2600 BCE and is 460 ft (140 m) high.

Key
1 Pyramid
2 Boat pits
3 Cemetery fields
4 Queen's pyramid
5 Mortuary temple
6 Causeway
7 Nobles' and courtiers' tombs
8 Valley temple
9 Nile River

© DIAGRAM

The ancient tombs of Nubia

The historical region of Nubia covered parts of present-day southern Egypt and northern Sudan, extending southward along the Nile from its first cataract (unnavigable stretch) almost as far as present-day Khartoum, the Sudanese capital.

Nubian civilizations

Several civilizations emerged in Nubia. The oldest known – and the oldest in sub-Saharan Africa – is the Kingdom of Kush, which began to emerge as early as 3200 BCE. Around 2400 BCE, Kush entered its period of expansion. Nine hundred years later, however, the Kingdom of Kush was conquered by Ancient Egypt. Pictures and statues of Nubians have been found in Ancient Egyptian tombs.

Around 920 BCE, a dynasty of Nubian kings in Napata began to govern, as the Kingdom of Nubia, independently from Egypt. Under King Piankhy (reigned 751–712 BCE), Egypt was conquered and Nubia reached its territorial zenith. These gains began to be lost to invading Assyrians during the reign of Taharqa (683–663 BCE). In 671 BCE, the Nubians lost control of most of Egypt including Memphis, the capital, and by 657 BCE they had lost it all to the Assyrians.

The Nubian capital was moved from Napata to Meroe in c. 300 BCE and the powerful Meroitic Kingdom emerged. Meroe became an important center of iron making. In 324 CE, the Meroitic Kingdom collapsed after being defeated by the Ethiopian Axumite Kingdom.

Ancient sites *(left)*
From 3200 BCE to 1500 CE, Nubian kingdoms flourished along the Nile River.
Key

NOBATIA	Kingdom
(Abu Simbel)	Modern city or town
●	Historical site
▦	Kush (1750 –1500 BCE)

Lion Temple *(below)*
The northern gateway of the Lion Temple at Naqa, showing Queen Amanitore smiting her foes. Built 2,000 years ago, this Meroitic temple is dedicated to the god *Apedemak*.

A	B	D	E	Ê	H̱ (KH)	Ḥ (KH)	I	K	L	M	N

Ñ	P	Q	R	S	Š (SH)	T	TE	TÊ	W	Y

Meroitic writing *(left)*
The people of Meroe developed their own alphabetical script, which used both characters and *hieroglyphs* (picture symbols).

Nubian crown

This silver and gold crown was found on the head of a Nubian king in a tomb at Ballana. It is identical to those worn by the royalty of Meroe, as depicted in ancient reliefs found in Sudan.

Modern Nubian house *(below)*

In painting this house, the Nubian artist has used emblems and symbols that date from historical Nubia. Until recently, descendants of the Nubians still lived in the region. After the building of Egypt's Aswan High Dam in the 1960s, however, much of Nubia was flooded and many Nubians were relocated in Sudan or Egypt.

After the fall of Meroe, Nubia broke up into three kingdoms: Nobatia; Makuria (or Makurra); and Alodia (or Alwa). Between 575 and 599, Makuria absorbed Nobatia and formed the larger kingdom of Dongola (or Dunqulah). This kingdom disappeared after Arabs invaded the region in the fifteenth century. Alodia collapsed in c. 1500 when it was overrun by the Funj Kingdom from farther south in present-day Sudan.

Archeological remains

Archeologists have discovered over one hundred ancient burial chambers of Nubian people. The earliest tombs date from c. 300–400 and were found at Qostol. The latest date from c. 500–550 and were found at Ballana. These sites are in present-day Egypt, just north of the second cataract of the Nile. They are attributed to Nubian civilizations that arose after the fall of Meroe — most likely the Nobatia Kingdom. The sites have since been flooded by the building of the Aswan High Dam.

The tombs were buried under mounds of earth from 7 to 40 ft (2–12 m) high. Under these mounds were the remains of mud-brick tombs. Many were obviously the graves of royalty; large numbers of people, horses, camels, and dogs had been put to death to accompany their masters and mistresses into the afterworld. The tombs were full of treasures — gold and silver jewelry, silverware and ironware, and many bronze articles including folding tables and chairs. The presence of many imported goods from Greece, Rome, and Egypt shows that the Nubians engaged in commerce with the rest of the world.

The Nubians were converted to Christianity in the sixth century and some of the later tombs contain Christian inscriptions. Archeologists have also found the ruins of a number of castles and early Christian churches. The Nubians mostly built their churches in brick, but a few were made of stone.

Dinka

T he Dinka are a Nilotic people who live in southern Sudan. There are just over one million Dinka in more than twenty different groups, making them the predominant people in southern Sudan.

History

Little is known of Dinka history before 1500, when they are known to have been settled in their present location.

RECENT EVENTS The north of Sudan and the Sudanese government have long been dominated by Arab culture and politics. Attempts to impose these on the largely non-Muslim, non-Arab south have often lead to conflict. As the largest and most widespread southern Sudanese people, the Dinka have often been at the forefront of these conflicts. In 1978, the Sudanese government began the construction of the Jonglei Canal in the south. The aim of the canal was to conserve water – a great deal is lost through evaporation as the Nile waters pass through the swampy Sudd region. The water saved could be used to irrigate agricultural land reclaimed from the Sudd. The canal was viewed with suspicion by many southerners, especially the Dinka, who saw it as an attempt to convert cattle-herding people like themselves to settled farming,

Dinka timeline	
c. 1000	Nilotic peoples settled in region to the far southwest of Bahr al Ghazal river
1500s	Dinka settled in present location. Different Dinka groups begin to emerge
1821	Trade routes opened from north to south; leading to reduced southern population through disease and slavery
1840s–1850s	Arab slave trade develops in Dinka territory
1882	Anglo-Egyptian force conquers Sudan; Mahdist campaigns against conquerors begin
1898	Anglo-Egyptian force conquers Mahdists; Sudan ruled as a joint British and Egyptian colony
1955–1972	First civil war between north and south Sudan
1956	Sudanese independence
1972	End of first Sudanese civil war; south granted regional autonomy
1978	Work on Jonglei Canal begins in southern Sudan
1983	Sudan adopts *Sharia* (Islamic holy) law against wishes of mainly non-Muslim south; civil war breaks out again
1984	Rebel raids on Jonglei Canal result in suspension of work
1988	Limited amount of work begins on Jonglei Canal
1990s	Despite many cease-fires, Sudan's civil war continues

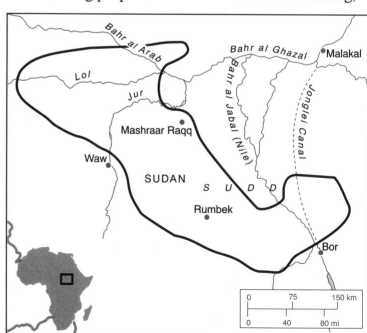

Sparring
Young Dinka men hone their fighting skills by engaging in mock battles using shields and fighting sticks or spears. Traditionally, these skills are deemed important as they are considered to reflect a man's ability to protect his home and family.

making them easier to control and govern. Furthermore, in 1983, the government divided the south into three regions to break up the power base of the Dinka. Finally, the adoption of *Sharia* (Islamic holy) law in 1983 led the southern Sudanese to rebel, and civil war broke out.

The southern-based rebel groups draw a lot of their support from the Dinka. The main rebel group was originally divided into two wings: military – the Sudanese People's Liberation Army (SPLA) – and political – the Sudanese People's Liberation Movement (SPLM). In 1988, the Sudanese government was accused by the SPLM and international human rights organizations of attempted genocide (extermination) of the Dinka. Rebel attacks led to work on the Jonglei Canal being suspended in 1984, and work has only partially been resumed since. By 1991, the SPLA controlled most of the south, but in the same year, it split into different factions. Reports have surfaced of civilians being forcibly conscripted by both the government and rebel groups. Despite several cease-fires, the civil war continues.

Pottery *(below)*
Clay pots are vital for cooking and carrying water and are usually made by women. Coils of clay are built up into the desired shape, then the edges are moistened and smoothed down. Color can be added by rubbing with a colored stone and patterns can be inscribed using a sharp tool. The pot is then fired by placing it overnight in a hole in the ground and covering it with burning straw and dung.

© DIAGRAM

Dinka headrest

The simple form of this wooden headrest enhances the natural shape of the wood. Many Dinka would have at least one of these pieces of furniture. They are used mainly as headrests for sleeping at night and are particularly useful for protecting elaborate hairstyles. Headrests can also be used as stools; it is not considered appropriate, for example, for elderly men to sit directly on the ground.

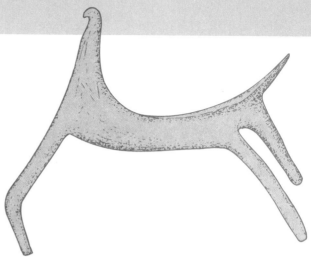

Fishing

This Dinka woman is fishing with a specially-designed cane trap. As the rainy season comes to an end, the swamps contract and fish are easily trapped in the shallow waters.

Language

The Dinka language is also called Dinka and belongs to the Nilotic language group.

Ways of life

SEMINOMADIC PASTORALISM The vast majority of Dinka practice *seminomadic pastoralism*, an activity they combine with growing crops. The region inhabited by the Dinka is largely *savanna* (grassland with scattered trees and shrubs), sloping down to the Sudd – a region of small streams and swamps that is subject to flooding in the rainy season. The year divides into two seasons: the dry season, which stretches from roughly November through April, and the rainy season, which can begin as early as March and last until October. In an apparently inhospitable land, the Dinka's lifestyle has been finely tuned over the years to cope with these changing seasons.

During the rainy season, most Dinka live in permanent settlements. These are built on slightly higher, more-wooded land in the savanna regions to avoid flooding. As the pastures around the villages dry out, the Dinka take their cattle and set up camps near rivers, where the floods have subsided and new grass has sprung up.

During the dry season, the permanent settlements will be virtually deserted by all but elderly people and nursing mothers. Too delicate to survive heavy rains, tobacco is the only crop grown during the dry season. It is mainly grown for sale in the market towns and provides an important source of cash with which to buy goods not produced within the community. Toward the end of the dry season, fishing festivals may be held. Trapped by the receding rivers, large numbers of fish are caught in designated pools that have been left untouched for this purpose. These events attract people from a wide area.

When the first rains come, the Dinka families begin to move back to the permanent settlements, and for the next few weeks they are busy tilling the soil and planting the seed for the next crops. Cereals, for example durra, corn, and millet, and vegetables such as pumpkin and okra, are grown. The main rainy season begins about June, and the rains bring floods with them. A few of the younger herders take the cattle off to drier pastures in the savanna, leaving most of the people to look after the growing crops. When the floods stop, some of the young men go home to help with the harvest, followed a few weeks later by the rest with the cattle.

CATTLE Cattle are central to the Dinka way of life. Owning cattle means wealth. In an environment of scarce resources, the Dinka do not use their animals just for food, which would be wasteful; cattle provide for a wide variety of the Dinka's material needs. Cow's milk is drunk or made into butter which, in turn, can be made into oil for cooking or anointing the skin. Cattle urine is used for washing, dyeing hair, and tanning hides. The

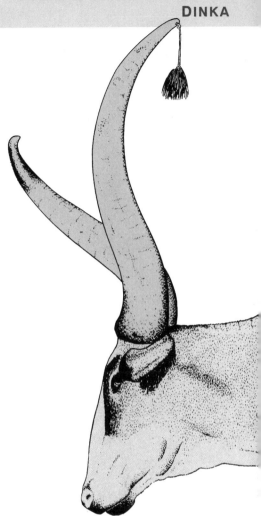

Song ox
Young Dinka men are usually given an ox after their initiation into manhood. The owner will often compose songs praising his ox. It is a Dinka custom to train the horns of these "song oxen" into special shapes and maybe decorate the tips with tassels.

Traditional dry-season home
The traditional Dinka dry-season home is ideally suited to both the Dinka's lifestyle and their environment – which has a few scattered savanna trees but little stone for building. These buildings are made from the plentiful savanna grass, which is dried and attached to a frame of flexible saplings. This type of house is easy to dismantle and carry from camp to village, where more permanent shelters are used.

© DIAGRAM

71

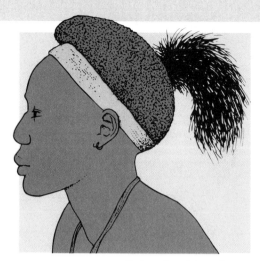

Hairstyles *(above)*
This picture shows a hairstyle worn by a young Dinka man, which has an ostrich feather attached to complete the style. The Dinka usually take great care of their hair. It may be cut, shaped, and set in place using cow dung and mud.

dung is used as fuel. The smoke and ash from dung-fires is used as an insect repellent. The ash is also used for body decoration and its fine abrasive quality makes it a good cleaning agent. If an animal dies – usually through old age or accident – every part is put to some use. The skins are made into leather for mats, drums, cloth, and ropes; the meat is eaten; and the horns and bones can be carved into tools or musical instruments.

Not surprisingly, the Dinka endow their cattle with great religious and social significance. Cattle are sacrificed in religious worship and can be used to make payments that settle disputes or seal alliances, or they can be given as *bridewealth* (a present made by the groom to his new wife's family) to legally confirm a marriage.

Social structure

SOCIAL STRUCTURE One Dinka group may have as many as 30,000 members. Every group has a number of subgroups, which comprise different extended families. The extended-family unit, or *clan,* includes all blood relatives and can number in the hundreds. Each of these clans is associated with a particular animal or plant. Clan members respect, and avoid harming, their own clan's particular emblem.

Personal art
This Dinka man and woman have patterns painted onto their faces using ash. The styles, patterns, and designs used for all forms of personal art depend on the taste of the wearer and are influenced by current fashions, which change every few years. Otherwise occupied by the current civil war, many personal art forms are in danger of falling into disuse among the Dinka.

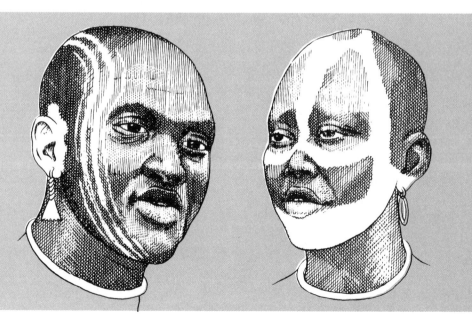

POLITICAL STRUCTURE Each group has a priestly or religious clan, called a *bany,* whose traditional role is to control and safeguard the land. The head of the bany is known as the *beng* – "Master of the Fishing Spear." His authority is always based more on persuasion and reputation than force. People will approach him to have their disputes settled and grievances aired. Since 1972, when southern Sudan was granted regional autonomy, the beng of a group has often been elected by the people to be the local political, as well as religious, leader.

Culture and religion

RELIGION Although some Dinka have converted to Christianity or Islam, the Dinka religion is still very much alive. It involves belief in a number of *yeeth* (divinities or powers). It is not always appropriate to define Dinka gods in a set way. For example, the widely-revered *yath* (singular of yeeth) *Nhialac* is several things: the sky; what is in the sky; an entity sometimes called "father" or "creator"; and also a power that can be possessed by any yeeth or even particular men. Another important yath is *Deng,* who is associated with rain, thunder, and lightning. *Garang* – associated with the Sun – was the first man, and *Abuk* – associated with rivers – the first woman. *Macardit* is the source of death and sterility. Other yeeth include the emblems of clans. New yeeth are adopted as groups come into contact with other Dinka groups.

PERSONAL ART Dinka people, the young in particular, use their own bodies as canvases onto which they create living art. Butter or oil made from milk or the fruit of the shea tree is used to anoint the body. Then friends paint designs onto each other's skin using a paint made from cattle-dung ash and water. The Dinka also shave, cut, and sculpt their hair into neat designs using cattle dung as a fixing gel; hair may also be dyed a dark orange color using the acidic urine of the cattle. The designs used are constantly developing over time and new ones adopted as each group comes into contact with other groups, gains new members, or undergoes various other changes. *Scarification* (in which permanent designs are created with scars) is also sometimes used to adorn the body.

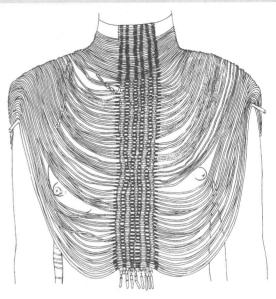

Beaded clothing
Traditionally, unmarried women wear bodices made of thousands of tiny, colored beads. These hang from the neck rather like very wide necklaces. Dinka men may also wear a similar garment: a kind of beaded corset. Beaded clothing is largely reserved for special occasions nowadays; imported or Western-style clothes and fabrics are more often worn on an everyday basis.

Tents to temples: buildings of North Africa

Urban homes

Houses in the cities and villages of northern North Africa are built on a pattern that is common to many parts of southwest Asia and the lands that border the Mediterranean Sea. Windows are small and, if the house is large enough to have an inner courtyard, more windows face onto that than onto the outside. A flat roof is standard; it serves as an extra room, which can be used as a sleeping place on hot nights. In regions with low rainfall, a pitched (sloping) roof is unnecessary. Some roofs have a simple one-room structure on top, which serves as a sort of penthouse.

Rural homes

Settled communities in the rural parts of the Maghreb (Morocco, Algeria, and Tunisia) build their homes in the general pattern of the coastal settlements, often single-storey with flat roofs. In the Sudan, however, some people make circular homes with conical thatched roofs – the Nuba, for example. It is common to find four or five of these around a covered courtyard, each with a different purpose such as living or sleeping quarters, storerooms, or shelter for animals.

Mobile homes

The nomads (herders who travel with their animals in search of pasture and water) of the Sahara Desert have to carry their shelters with them wherever they go. Most nomad shelters are tents. The standard design of tents varies considerably from one ethnic group to another. Every tent, however, consists of a framework, generally of light poles, supporting a covering of cloth, matting, leather, or plastic sheeting. Some tents have a covering made of grass or palm fronds. Guy ropes attached to pegs hold the tent up in the ordinary way. Tents are usually pitched facing south or with the rear (closed) end toward the prevailing wind. The main requirement for all these portable shelters is that they can be easily taken down and stowed in loads for animals such as the camel to carry.

Tekna tent (below)
The Tekna are a nomadic people who live in southwest Morocco. The framework of their peaked tents comprises two tapered poles; these are covered with cloth, which is pegged into place. The floor is then covered with matting.

Modern architecture (right)
The finance ministry building in Tunis, the capital of Tunisia, has been built in a style that incorporates elements of traditional Arabic architecture with up-to-date building techniques. The result is a distinctive modern building.

Dinka wet-season home (right)
During the rainy season, the *seminomadic* Dinka people of southern Sudan live in homes raised above ground level. This traditional cylindrical home has *wattle-and-daub* walls and a roof thatched with grass.

Nubian architecture (above)
This crumbling Nubian temple is made from stone blocks and shows the influence of Ancient Egyptian architecture. Many Nubian kingdoms flourished along the Nile River in present-day Sudan between 3200 BCE and 1500 CE.

Building materials

The traditional material for building in North Africa is mud brick. People make mud bricks by hand or in molds, and set them in the sun to dry. The mortar used to bind the bricks together is also mud. The builders finish the walls with a coating of clay, mud, or lime mortar, which can then be whitewashed. This hard coating protects the walls from rain. In places where rain is regular, an overhanging roof of thatch screens the walls. The Romans introduced kiln-baked bricks to North Africa, and some bricks of this type are used today. In some places builders use stone, and preformed concrete blocks are now common. For important structures, such as temples and palaces, the ancient Romans, Egyptians, and Carthaginians used stone. In Sudan, some people build their homes with wattle-and-daub – *a woven latticework of sticks thickly plastered with clay. Roofs are built of timber – often just a framework covered with thatch. Cloth for tents is woven from a variety of materials, including camel's and goat's hair and sheep's wool; sheepskins or goatskins are also used. Wood is in short supply in most parts of North Africa, so it is used sparingly.*

Religious buildings

The majority of religious buildings in North Africa are the mosques of Islam. Non-Islamic religious buildings do survive, however, from North Africa's pre-Islamic period. In Egypt, there are temples built by the Ancient Egyptians and tombs built to house their dead – the pyramids, some of the most famous buildings in the world. Christian Coptic churches also exist in Egypt dating from the historical Coptic Period to the present day. Roman and Carthaginian temples have also been found in the northern coastal areas that these people once colonized.

Bedouin granary *(below)*
This mud and clay structure in Tunisia was originally built by *nomadic* Bedouin Arabs. It is called a *gorfa*, and was used by the Bedouin as a *granary* (a building for storing grain). This gorfa now provides housing for a previously homeless family.

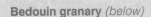

Nuba

The Nuba live in the Nuba Hills of Kordofan province, southern Sudan. This region lies west of the White Nile River and south of Khartoum, the Sudanese capital. There are more than 500,000 Nuba, and they fall into more than sixty groups and many more subgroups. (The Nuba should not be confused with the Nubians, who originate from the region now covered by Lake Nasser.)

History

Although very little is known about Nuba history until the Arab invasion of North Africa in the seventh century, it seems they have lived in their present location for centuries. Three hundred years before the Arab invasion, references had already been made to the presence of people called the "Black Noba," who were probably ancestors of the modern Nuba. Some Nuba groups claim to have always lived in the Nuba Hills. Since the eighteenth century, others have moved up into the inaccessible hills in retreat from Baggara raids or, in the late nineteenth century, Mahdist troops.

Nuba timeline

300s	"Black Noba," probable ancestors of present-day Nuba, recorded in southern Sudan
640	Arabs begin conquest of North Africa; Islam introduced
1700s	Arab slave raids against the Nuba. Baggara raids begin; more Nuba retreat into hills
1821	Trade routes opened from north to south Sudan – as a result, southern population is reduced by disease and slave trading
1882	Anglo-Egyptian forces conquer Sudan; Mahdi begins campaigns; more Nuba retreat into hills
1898	Anglo-Egyptian force conquers Mahdist State
1955	First civil war between south and north Sudan begins
1956	Sudanese independence
1972	South granted regional autonomy; first civil war ends
1975	Chevron begins drilling for oil in southern Sudan
1983	Sudan adopts *Sharia* (Islamic holy) law against wishes of mainly non-Muslim south; civil war breaks out again
1983– 1996	Many Nuba join Sudanese People's Liberation Army (SPLA), a southern-based rebel group
1986	Chevron pulls out of Sudan
1990s	Famine hits Nuba Hills. Reports of "ethnic cleansing" of the Nuba by Baggara militias
1992	Relocation camps for Nuba, so-called "peace villages," set up by government

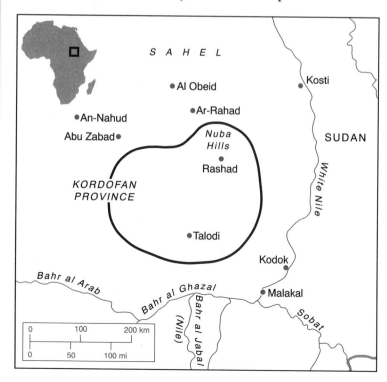

RECENT EVENTS During the lengthy Sudanese civil war between the Islamic north and the mainly non-Muslim south, the Nuba have been drawn into conflicts with their Islamic neighbors, the Baggara. The government has armed the Baggara, which has resulted in thousands of Nuba being killed. Many thousands more have been deported from the hills to government-run "peace villages," where they are under pressure to convert to Islam or to join the government troops fighting the southern rebels. Reports of rebel groups forcibly conscripting civilians have also surfaced.

Language

The Nuba speak over fifty different languages of the Koalib, Tegali, Talodi, Tumtum, and Katla groups of the Niger-Kordofanian language family.

Ways of life

Most Nuba are farmers and live in permanent settlements. They cultivate the land with spadelike hoes, and terrace and irrigate their fields. Common crops are millet, sorghum, and corn. Other crops

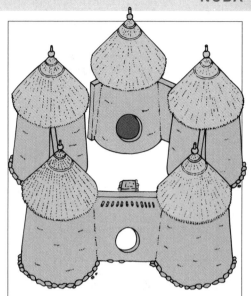

Traditional Nuba architecture
Structures called *tukls* – with thatched, cone-shaped roofs – are traditional Nuba buildings. Each tukl is connected by mud walls with several others, and the tukls surround a courtyard to form an individual family's complex. Several of these complexes clustered together form a community. The ongoing civil war, forcible relocations, and the development of new building techniques have made these distinctly Nuba buildings less common.

Cicatrix
Some Nuba men and women have elaborate patterns on their faces and bodies, produced by scar tissue called *cicatrix*.

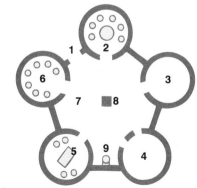

Key

1 Entrance	**5** Grinding stone
2 Granary	**6** Storage tukl
3 Sleeping tukl	**7** Courtyard
4 Shelter for animals	**8** Cooking area
	9 Shower

© DIAGRAM

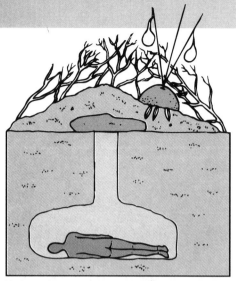

Nuba grave

Traditionally, the Nuba bury their dead in individual tombs. A hole is dug with a very narrow entrance and the body is laid on its side, facing east with its head pointing north. A mound of earth covers a stone over the entrance, and objects such as water-filled gourds and cattle horns are placed on the mound to help the deceased in the afterlife.

Dung bowls

These bowls were made by Nuba artisans from animal dung and water, which have been made into a paste and molded by hand. The patterns are similar to those used to decorate Nuba homes. Vessels like this may have been used in wedding ceremonies and were part of a girl's collection of items with which she would enter marriage.

include cotton, gourds, melons, okra, onions, cucumbers, peppers, and sesame. The Nuba also keep cattle and goats, which provide milk, and chickens, donkeys, horses, and sheep. Except in the few Muslim subgroups, many Nuba also raise pigs.

Normally, men work on the land and milk the cattle and goats, while women look after the chickens and pigs and gather wild foods such as nuts. Women also work in the fields to help with harvesting.

In the 1970s, oil companies began drilling in the oil-rich south of Sudan. Many Nuba men were employed by the companies. Since the outbreak of the civil war, however, exploitation has largely ceased and job opportunities in the industry have dried up.

HOMES The traditional Nuba home is a cylindrical mud structure with a cone-shaped thatched roof. Entrances are generally keyhole shaped. Home to a family may consist of five of these grouped around a courtyard. In towns scattered around the Nuba Hills, where many of the administrative centers are, the Nuba work and live in flat-roofed buildings of brick or stone.

Social structure

Nuba society has been drastically affected by the decade-long civil war. Many people have been killed during the conflict and a large proportion of Nuba men and boys have been forcibly conscripted into either the rebel armies or government troops. With many Nuba living in the so-called "peace villages" or in refugee camps in neighboring countries such as Zaire and the Central African Republic, Nuba social structures, which differ from group to group but are generally based around *clans* (several extended families linked by a common ancestor or ancestors, in this case often a woman) are gradually being dismantled.

Culture and religion

RELIGION The majority of the Nuba follow the Nuba religion, which differs in nature from group to group. A minority of Nuba are Christians, however, and an even smaller proportion are Muslims.

PERSONAL ART The Nuba are famous for their elaborate forms of personal art, which involve scarring and painting their bodies. The patterns used to decorate the skin are rich in symbolism. Both men and women have this decorative scarring, but for women it denotes important milestones, and the scarring process continues for many years. The skin is cut in patterns and then rubbed with ash, saliva, or sesame oil. The first scarring is done in childhood or at the start of puberty, and the final scarring takes place after a woman has weaned her first child. The scars fade with age and become less prominent. As the Nuba are otherwise occupied by the current civil war, however, many peronal art forms are in danger of falling into disuse.

WRESTLING A popular social activity among the Nuba is wrestling. Boys begin their training at the age of thirteen or fourteen. From that time onward, a boy ideally spends at least half his time at a camp where he learns and practices wrestling. As he progresses, he passes through four grades. Each grade has a belt or sash. White is the lowest grade; the belts of higher grades are made of colored cloth or goatskin, with a cow's tail as a badge of rank. The most accomplished wrestlers adorn their belts with brass bells. A wrestler paints his body with patterns in yellow or white. He also shaves his head and smears it with ashes mixed with milk. Nowadays, however, few can spare time for wrestling in the midst of a civil war.

Wrestling
Wrestling is a popular sport and is taken very seriously. Bouts can be fierce, but end when one wrestler pins his opponent's shoulders to the ground. In more peaceful times, huge crowds attended matches and skillful wrestlers could draw people from miles around; many wrestlers became celebrities whose fame was widespread.

© DIAGRAM

Hair: styles and symbolism

For many North Africans, hairstyles have traditionally been symbolic as well as decorative, for both men and women. Hairstyling is a professional, demanding skill, mostly practiced by women though sometimes by men as well. It is also an art, one that is handed down through generations, and it can be a form of self-expression, even of sculpture. But self-expression is only one of the reasons why hairdressing is so important among many African peoples. Hair, and the ability to control it, has great symbolic significance. The Nuba of southern Sudan, for instance, believe that shaving and grooming one's hair is what distinguishes humans from animals — it is a kind of control that animals cannot practice.

Traditional beliefs about hairstyling

The Nuba have many other traditional beliefs about hair. Among the Nuba, only men decorate their hair, although traditionally both men and women oil their hair and dress it with ocher (a reddish brown or yellow clay). Also, women won't groom their hair while they are pregnant and many women shave their hair after they have reached an age when they can no longer have babies. Hair grooming is an essential aspect of being part of society; when outside the normal society — for example, when some members of a village go to farms away from their village to wait for the grain to ripen — the Nuba don't groom their hair. The hair itself is also significant; hair cuttings must be buried to prevent them being stepped on by another, otherwise misfortune could result.

Historically in many African cultures, the way the hair was presented or styled signified a certain role in society or the passing of an important milestone. For example, among peoples living in the Maghreb (Algeria, Morocco, and Tunisia), puberty for both girls and boys was marked with new hairstyles. For many Africans of the southern Sudan area, hairstyle

Berber styles
There are many variations of Berber hairstyles. Among the Berber people who live in the Middle Atlas Mountains of north Morocco, a common hairstyle *(left, top)* involves braiding the hair down the back. Then an elaborate scarf is wrapped around the hair like a turban and held in place with cords. Elsewhere, young Berber girls may have their hair cut into a skullcap shape close to the head *(left, center).* A "knot" of hair, which is decorated with ribbons and other ornaments, is left to hang down on one side.

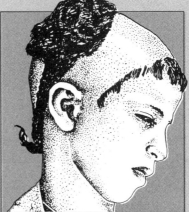

Giving messages with hair
This Toposa woman from southern Sudan is wearing her hair in lots of tiny pigtails to show that she is married.

can still indicate the wearer's status in society. The use of hairstyles to distinguish people according to status is, however, less common than it was, as personal preference and fashion increasingly dictate which hairstyle a person chooses. Practices such as shaving one's head (to signify that a woman has passed childbearing age), or covering the hair with a headdress (to signify that a woman is married), still maintain their traditional meanings in some places. Hair grooming is also a practical concern, especially for warriors; long hair can be dangerous and easy for the enemy to grab hold of. As in most parts of the world, special occasions still demand that extra attention is paid to the hair.

Techniques and materials

Techniques used in hairstyling include braiding and weaving, threading fibers or beads onto the hair, and molding the hair into shapes using clay as a fixing gel. Some elaborate styles can take several hours to create. Different regions and different ethnic groups reflect a wide variety of styles and techniques, and a variety of dressing agents are used. In some parts, ocher is rubbed on the hair to give it an interesting texture and color; among other people, fat or oil is used; and still others use beeswax to coat the hair. Most styling aids are made using locally available ingredients.

Braids

This Tuareg girl has divided her hair into several braids. This style is both practical, as it keeps long hair under control, and attractive.

Colorful hair
In preparation for a dance, this Moorish woman from Morocco has had her hair done in several long, thin braids, which have been interwoven with colorful beads and glass balls.

False hair
A traditional custom among the Jewish women of Morocco's past involved combining false hair – made from cows' tails or wool – with real hair. This example uses wool wound into hornlike shapes and attached on both sides of the head to hang behind the shoulders.

Dinka fashion
This young Dinka man from southern Sudan is having an ostrich feather attached to his hair by a friend. His hair has been colored red with *ocher* and then shaved close to the head in the shape of a bowl.

Nuer

The Nuer are a Nilotic people who live in southern Sudan. The Nuer are closely related to the Dinka, another Nilotic group. There are about 300,000 Nuer.

History

Along with other Nilotic peoples, the Nuer originated in a region to the southwest of their present location. Over the years, they migrated to their present location. This gradual process of migration was forced to halt when the British and Egyptians conquered Sudan in 1898. After Sudan achieved independence, an ongoing civil war tore the country apart; many Nuer temporarily fled to neighboring countries, and their herds were drastically reduced. This civil war ended in 1972, after the south, an area populated by many different ethnic groups, was given regional autonomy.

RECENT EVENTS In 1983, the Sudanese government adopted *Sharia* (Islamic holy) law, and triggered another civil war between the Muslim north and the largely non-Muslim south. By the 1990s, the main rebel groups had split into many different, often warring,

Nuer timeline

c. 1000	Nilotic peoples settled in region to the far southwest of Bahr al Ghazal river
c. 1700s	Nuer people begin to migrate eastward
1821	Trade routes opened from north to south Sudan, leading to a reduced southern population through disease and slave trading
1840s–1850s	Arab slave trade develops in Nuer territory; Nuer are targeted by slave raiders
c. 1850	Active period of eastward Nuer migrations begin
1898	Britain and Egypt colonize Sudan. Boundaries between Nuer and Dinka fixed
1955–1972	First Sudanese civil war between north and south
1956	Sudanese independence
1972	End of first Sudanese civil war; south granted regional autonomy
1975	Chevron begins drilling for oil in southern Sudan
1983	Sudan adopts *Sharia* (Islamic holy) law against wishes of mainly non-Muslim south; civil war breaks out again
1986	Chevron pulls out of Sudan
1990s	Despite many cease-fires, the civil war continues
1996	Rebel groups warn foreign oil companies not to return to southern Sudan after reports of planned investment

factions. The Nuer-dominated South Sudan Independence Movement (SSIM) is often in conflict with the mainly-Dinka Sudanese People's Liberation Army (SPLA). Despite many cease-fires, the civil war still continues in Sudan today. Attacks on civilians are common and Nuer civilians have been forcibly conscripted into both rebel and government troops.

Language

The Nuer language is also called Nuer and belongs to the Nilotic language group.

Ways of life

SEMINOMADIC PASTORALISM The vast majority of Nuer are *seminomadic pastoralists* who rear cattle, an activity they combine with growing crops. The Nuer live in a region that is largely *savanna* (grasslands with scattered tree and shrubs), but some of their land is in the Sudd – a seasonally swampy region. During the rainy season, from May to December, the pastures

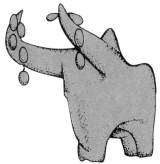

Clay oxen
These ox figures, made from clay with tassels hanging from their horns, symbolize the important role cattle have in Nuer culture.

© DIAGRAM

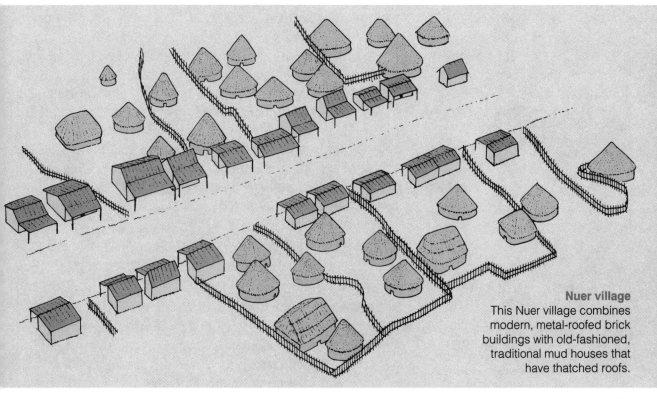

Nuer village
This Nuer village combines modern, metal-roofed brick buildings with old-fashioned, traditional mud houses that have thatched roofs.

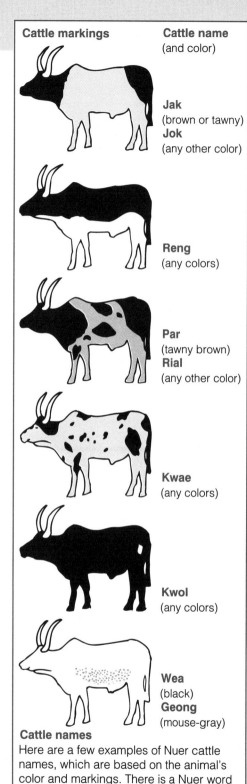

Cattle markings

Cattle name
(and color)

Jak
(brown or tawny)
Jok
(any other color)

Reng
(any colors)

Par
(tawny brown)
Rial
(any other color)

Kwae
(any colors)

Kwol
(any colors)

Wea
(black)
Geong
(mouse-gray)

Cattle names
Here are a few examples of Nuer cattle names, which are based on the animal's color and markings. There is a Nuer word for any of the many possible variations.

around the rivers flood and become uninhabitable swamps. This is the time when the Nuer move to settlements on higher ground. During this season, the women cultivate crops such as peanuts, millet, and corn, while the men graze their herds nearby. As the swamps dry out during the dry season, from January to May, the Nuer men and their herds follow the receding rivers to new pastures.

In the 1970s, drilling for oil by the US company Chevron brought trucks and bulldozers to Nuer territory. Many Nuer took work on oil rigs. Production was stopped indefinitely in 1986, however, after several Chevron employees were kidnapped and murdered by rebels. Although the lifestyle of many Nuer was altered from seminomadic pastoralism to wage-labor, the work brought in much-needed cash for families and villages.

CATTLE Cattle are central to the Nuer way of life and are rarely killed for their meat alone. Cows are important as they provide milk; the Nuer milk-based diet is supplemented by some fishing and hunting. Cattle are important in many other ways. The prestige of the head of the household is determined by the size of the herd owned by the family. Cattle are sometimes sacrificed in religious rituals, and they are presented by the groom to his bride's family upon marriage. Young men often take a name based on the color of their favorite bull.

Because of their major role in Nuer culture, cattle are often the source of conflict; a cow owned by one man might eat the crops of another, for instance. They are also often the means of resolving conflicts, however, and not just those caused by cattle. Serious disputes are referred to the *kuuarmuon* (the chief and local magistrate) who determines the appropriate compensation, which is often a payment of cattle.

Social structure

SOCIAL ORGANIZATION The Nuer are organized into many *clans,* which are extended families that share a common founding ancestor or ancestors. Territory and other resources are divided by clans. Members of a particular clan do not marry one another.

MARRIAGE Upon marriage, the Nuer, like many African people, practice a system called *bridewealth*, which involves a gift – usually cattle – given by the bridegroom to the bride's family. An ideal arrangement might be a gift of forty cows to be given to the father of the bride-to-be; these would then be distributed to the bride's relatives. Few can afford this amount while they are at war, however. Bridewealth does not represent payment for the woman, but compensation for her family's loss of a working member and is considered a token of respect. Marriages are only considered legal once the bridewealth has been received in full.

Children are important in that they link the families of their mother and father. This is believed to reduce the potential conflicts between families because they share an interest in the child's well-being. In Nuer eyes a marriage is not finalized until the woman has given birth to at least two children. This, combined with the fact that it may take many years to complete the bridewealth, makes Nuer marriages a lengthy process.

Nuer couples can divorce, but bridewealth complicates this if there are children. With no children, the bride's family returns all the bridewealth, and the couple is free to divorce and remarry. If the couple has had only one child, the husband can ask for the bridewealth to be returned, but some will be retained by the bride's family in exchange for the one child, who remains part of the husband's family. If more children are born, the bride's family will be justified in retaining more or all of the bridewealth, making divorce an expensive option for the husband.

Culture and religion

RELIGION Although some Nuer have converted to Christianity, the vast majority follow the Nuer religion, which is centered around a creator-god called *Kowth*. The Nuer pray to Kowth for health and good fortune and offer sacrifices of cattle. There is no organized hierarchy of religious officials, though some people act as diviners and healers. According to Nuer religion, the first Nuer, *Dja-gay*, came out of a hole in the ground.

Scarification
People of both sexes decorate their faces and bodies with scarring, though this traditional custom is becoming less common. The six lines on the man's forehead would have been made after his initiation into manhood – they are considered to be a mark of Nuer identity.

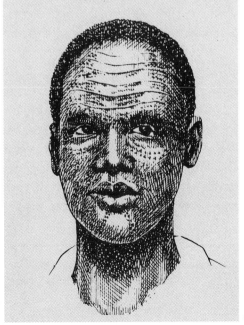

© DIAGRAM

Bridewealth and other marriage customs

Marriage is a serious business in all societies. Among most North African peoples, marriage is regarded as a tie between two families; it is not just the concern of the individuals involved. The majority of people in North Africa follow the Islamic religion. In general, they obey the Muslim laws on marriage, but with regional variations according to local customs. The non-Muslim people of southern Sudan, however, largely follow their own customs.

Muslim marriages

Islam does not prescribe any particular wedding ceremonies, but Muslim marriages are generally celebrated in style. Customs vary in detail from one ethnic group to another. One that is very common involves the bride having parts of her body painted with designs in henna, a reddish-brown dye made from the henna plant. The henna is applied especially to the hands. Often the bride's attendants decorate her with elaborate patterns on her arms and legs, and even on her face. Before the painting, the bride has a ceremonial bath. Usually, a qadi (a Muslim judge) performs the actual legal part of the ceremony. Elaborate feasting follows. In some groups, men and women hold separate feasts.

Under Islamic law, a man may have as many as four wives, but only if he is sufficiently well off to support them all equally. Each wife normally has her own home. Although most Tuareg are Muslims, polygyny (the practice of having more than one wife) is not widely practiced as it goes against the Tuareg's own monogamous (the practice or state of having only one marriage partner) traditions and few Tuareg women are tolerant of co-wives.

Divorce is simple for men: a man may end a marriage at will, and need not ask a court of law for a divorce. A woman can also divorce her husband, but generally has to pay a fee or go to court to do so. A couple can also divorce by mutual consent.

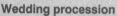

Wedding procession
This Egyptian bride is riding on a camel to the home of the groom accompanied by her friends, family, and some musicians. She sits beneath a decorative canopy, topped by waving palm fronds. Elaborate processions such as this one are customary only in rural, Islamic areas.

Bridewealth

A widespread custom is that of bridewealth, which is given by the bridegroom to the bride's family. The bride is not regarded as property; the payment is usually considered to be compensation to the bride's family for the loss of a working member. Part of it may be used by the couple to set up home together.

Among the Berbers and other groups whose living depends on herding animals, the fee is generally in the form of cattle or sheep. For the Nuer, for instance, the standard amount is generally between twenty and forty head of cattle; for the Dinka, the standard amount is between thirty and forty. Local circumstances affect these ideal figures, though. Nuer, Dinka, and Shilluk marriages are not considered legal until the bridewealth has been exchanged.

The bride's father distributes the cattle among her relatives, including uncles and aunts. There are strict rules for this distribution. Among some southern Sudanese ethnic groups, the bridegroom has to perform work for his prospective father-in-law. In farming communities such as the Nuba, this service takes the form of several days' work tilling the ground, or doing other necessary farm tasks.

If a husband divorces his wife, her family may have to pay back at least part of the bridewealth. This can make divorce difficult.

Choosing partners

In all strands of North African society, arranged marriages are traditionally more common than those in which men and women are free to choose partners for themselves. Individuals are increasingly more likely to make their own arrangements now than in the past, however.

In many ethnic groups, certain partnerships are chosen above all others. Marriage between cousins is often favored, especially cousins on the father's side. In some groups, such as the Beja, a man may marry his brother's widow, or the sister of his deceased wife. Among the Dinka, if the widow of a childless marriage remarries, her subsequent children are deemed to be those of her late husband.

Bride-to-be
The face of a Berber bride in the Atlas Mountains of Morocco is typically hidden by a highly decorated headdress.

One Berber group, the Ait Haddidou of Morocco, holds an annual bride fair. Men seeking wives and women seeking husbands flock to this three-day event. Many of the women are divorced; women are free to divorce as often as they like and can choose whom they wish to remarry. Relatives help men and women to choose their spouses at the fair.

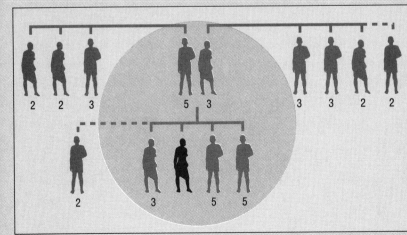

2 2 3   5 3   3 3 2 2

2   3 5 5

An example of bridewealth distribution
Among the Nuer in Sudan, up to forty head of cattle may be given to the bride's father by the groom's family. The father then distributes the cattle to his family. The immediate family – parents and siblings – is shown in the circle in the diagram, as is the bride (indicated by a dark tint) Members of the extended family – shown outside the circle – also receive cattle. They include aunts, uncles, and even – in this case – a half-brother and a half-uncle (attached by dotted lines). The numbers under each figure indicate the number of cattle received by that person.

Shilluk

The Shilluk are a Nilotic people who live in southern Sudan, along the banks of the White Nile River. There are roughly 120,000 Shilluk.

History

According to Shilluk history, their Nilotic ancestors began to migrate into their present-day location roughly four hundred years ago. Much of Shilluk history is preserved orally, through legends and stories, and goes back hundreds of years.

RECENT EVENTS With its ethnic and religious diversity, Sudan has suffered internal conflict for many years. Like the Sudanese Dinka, Nuer, Nuba, and many other southern groups, the Shilluk are non-Muslim minorities in a country in which Muslim Arabs from the north dominate the government. In 1983, the imposition of *Sharia* (Islamic holy) law triggered the outbreak of civil war between north and south Sudan.

In 1989, at least seven hundred Shilluk – mostly farmhands working roughly 100 miles (160 km) north of Kodok on the White Nile – were massacred by an Arab militia that had been armed by the government.

Shilluk timeline

c. 1000	Nilotic peoples are known to be settled in region to the far southwest of the Bahr al Ghazal river
c. 1500s	Nilotic ancestors of Shilluk migrate into present location along banks of White Nile
1684	Shilluk attacks on Arab settlements
1821	Trade routes opened from north to south Sudan, leading to a reduced southern population through disease and slave trading
1840s–1850s	Arab slave trade at height in Shilluk territory; Shilluk are targeted by slave raiders
1898	Britain and Egypt jointly colonize Sudan
1955–1972	First Sudanese civil war between north and south
1956	Sudanese independence
1972	End of first Sudanese civil war; south granted regional autonomy
1983	Sudan adopts *Sharia* (Islamic holy) law against wishes of mainly non-Muslim south; civil war breaks out again
1989	Over seven hundred Shilluk massacred at Jebelein
1990s	Despite many cease-fires, the civil war in Sudan continues. Reports of forcible conscriptions into both the rebel and government troops surface

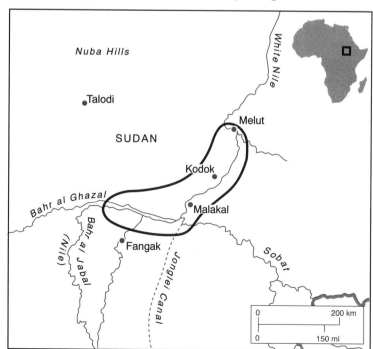

Language

The Shilluk speak a Nilotic language, which is also called Shilluk. Recently, Arabic has been imposed in schools and government-controlled areas.

Ways of life

The majority of Shilluk are *pastoralists* who combine the herding of cattle, sheep, and goats with growing crops. Beans, corn, millet, sesame, and pumpkins are common food crops and tobacco is grown both to use and to sell. Living along the banks of the White Nile River, fishing is an important activity for the Shilluk and fish are an important supplement to the diet. Shilluk fishermen intensively exploit the Nile waters for fish, which are caught with nets or specially designed fishing spears. Infrequent hunting parties are arranged by Shilluk men, though only smaller mammals – certain antelopes and gazelles, for example – are caught. In the past, hippopotamuses were hunted by the Shilluk, but they are now protected by law.

Social structure

SOCIAL STRUCTURE The Shilluk are divided into about one hundred *clans* or groups, each with a common ancestor or ancestors. The clans are scattered throughout various villages. Each village has an original or founding family called a *diel*.
POLITICAL STRUCTURE Each village has a chief, who is usually a member of the diel, subject to approval by the Shilluk king, or *reth*. The shilluk reth is a living symbol of Shilluk history and culture and is thought to be

King's residence
The palace of the Shilluk *reth,* or king, stands on an artificial mound of earth.

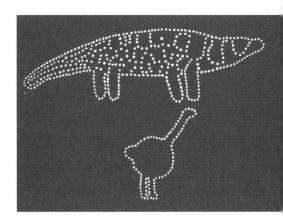

Shrine painting
This picture of a crocodile and ostrich is painted onto the wall of a shrine dedicated to the legendary founder of the Shilluk people – *Nyikang.* The crocodile is an important figure in the Shilluk religion. Some legends say that Nyikang's mother was a crocodile, or at least part crocodile, and the Shilluk make offerings to her at riverbanks.

89

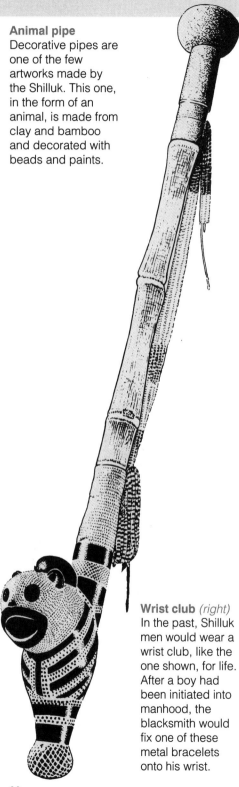

Animal pipe
Decorative pipes are one of the few artworks made by the Shilluk. This one, in the form of an animal, is made from clay and bamboo and decorated with beads and paints.

possessed by the spirit of *Nyikang* – the first Shilluk king and Shilluk culture hero. Nyikang is closely associated with the Shilluk religion. The reth is, therefore, sometimes described as a divine king. Indeed, the reth's role is more religious than political. He is the central figure who unites the Shilluk into a people. His subjects believe he is the reincarnation of the legendary Nyikang and that his good health ensures their prosperity. The reth resides at Kodok, formerly known as Fashoda. Since 1956, the reth has had the status of magistrate within the Sudanese judiciary.

Many traditions surround the ceremony of electing a new reth. The new ruler must be the son of any former king who can win the support of the people. The successful candidate is chosen by the two paramount chiefs. An electoral college of fourteen other chiefs has to approve their choice. There follow ceremonies at which effigies of Nyikang and his son *Dak* are paraded. Finally, the new king is enthroned, when it is believed that the spirit of Nyikang enters him.

Culture and religion

RELIGION Although a tiny minority of Shilluk people have converted to Islam, the vast majority adhere to the Shilluk religion. The Shilluk religion is centered around a creator-god known as *Juok*. Nyikang is considered to be the intermediary between an individual and Juok.

Wrist club *(right)*
In the past, Shilluk men would wear a wrist club, like the one shown, for life. After a boy had been initiated into manhood, the blacksmith would fix one of these metal bracelets onto his wrist.

Forehead scarring
The distinctive scarring on the forehead of this Shilluk man resembles beads stretching from temple to temple. He sports a very old-fashioned hairstyle, which resembles a helmet and has been formed by training and sculpting the hair.

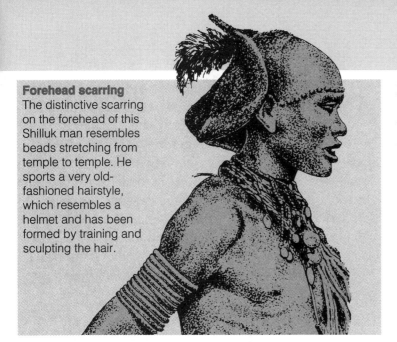

Shilluk man (right)
The Shilluk are a Nilotic people. This is a cultural and linguistic grouping that also includes the Dinka and Nuer. Nilotic people are often tall in stature. Shilluk men average between 6 and 7 ft (1.8–2.1 m) tall.

Whereas Nyikang founded the Shilluk people, it was Juok who created the world and who continues to maintain it. Also, whereas Nyikang is represented by a human – the reth – Juok is not.

The Shilluk have a wealth of stories about Nyikang. According to one legend, Nyikang came from the south sometime in the 1500s accompanied by his warrior son, Dak, and their followers. Using his powers, Nyikang helped his followers cross the crocodile-infested waters of the White Nile. Another legend says that Nyikang's mother was a crocodile, which may explain his power over these guardians of the river. Nyikang's mother is associated with rivers and river creatures, and offerings are left for her on riverbanks. In another legend, Nyikang fought with the Sun, which had gained possession of one of his cows, and drove it back into the sky. When the rains come at the end of the dry season, Nyikang is said to be overcoming the Sun and bringing much-needed water to the thirsty land.

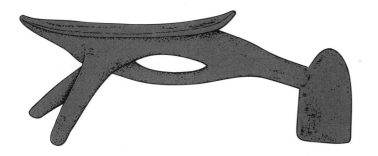

Headrest (left)
Headrests, such as the one shown here, are carved from wood, often in the shapes of animals or birds. The Shilluk believe the headrest was invented by *Nyikang*, their founder. They were generally used by Shilluk men while they slept so that their hair, which in the past was often elaborately styled, would not be ruined.

© DIAGRAM

Tuareg

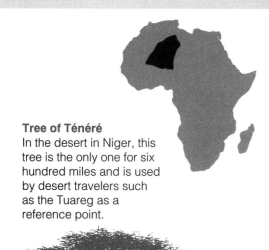

Tree of Ténéré
In the desert in Niger, this tree is the only one for six hundred miles and is used by desert travelers such as the Tuareg as a reference point.

The Tuareg (or Kel Tamacheq or Kel Tagelmust) are Berber in origin. Most live in and around the Sahara Desert from Algeria and Libya in the north to northern Nigeria and Mali in the south. This area covers a variety of terrains including desert and semidesert, mountainous regions in southern Algeria, and *savanna* (grasslands with scattered tress and shrubs). The southern part of Tuareg territory is in the Sahel – a strip of semidesert south of the Sahara – and in the savannas to its south. The vast majority of the Tuareg inhabit the Sahel. There are probably between one and three million Tuareg.

History

About 5,000 years ago, the Berber ancestors of the Tuareg lived along the North African coast of the Mediterranean, probably in present-day Libya. Since the seventh-century Arab invasion of North Africa, the Tuareg have traveled southward in a series of migrations. A proud and independent people, they fought with Arab, Turkish, and European invaders over the years. Arabs had conquered all of North Africa by 711, however, and the Tuareg were driven south into the desert.

Tuareg timeline

3000 BCE	Berber ancestors of Tuareg settled on the Mediterranean coast of North Africa
c. 100	Camels are introduced to North Africa
640 CE	Arab invasion and conquest of North Africa begins
711	Arabs control North Africa
1400s	Sultanate of Aïr established
1500s	Aïr loses its independence to Songhay Empire then to Kanem-Borno Empire
1600s	Aïr independent again
1800	Aïr reaches greatest extent
1899	First French military expedition against the Tuareg
1900	Aïr part of French West Africa
1917	Tuareg rebel against French
1954	Algerian war of independence
1960	Niger and Mali independent
1962	Algerian independence
1990s	Tuareg uprisings in both Niger and Mali
1994	Tuareg rebels sign peace accord in Niger
1995	Tuareg end uprising in Mali

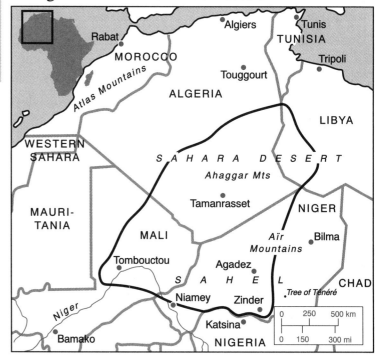

In the fifteenth century, the Sultanate of Aïr emerged as a centralized Tuareg state with its capital at Agades (modern Agadez) in present-day Niger. Aïr's wealth was based on control of the trans-Saharan trade routes. Great Tuareg trading *caravans* (companies of travelers) crossed the Sahara bringing gold, ivory, ostrich feathers, and slaves from West Africa to the Mediterranean coast. Southbound caravans carried salt and Arab and European goods to West Africa. Agades was part of the Songhay Empire from 1501–32 and was tributary to the Kanem-Borno Empire from 1532 until the 1600s. After attacking Borno, Aïr greatly expanded its territory at the expense of neighboring states during the seventeenth and eighteenth centuries. In the 1800s, the Sultanate of Aïr reached its greatest extent and Agades became an important political center in the region. By 1870, however, Agades had ceased to be of political importance and by 1900 Aïr had become part of the French West Africa colony.

COLONIALISM In 1917, a Tuareg rebellion against French rule was harshly suppressed. Many were killed and others (around 30,000) fled to northern Nigeria. By the 1960s, North and West Africa were independent from colonial rule, but the Tuareg found themselves divided up between various different nations that had no relevance to their history, lifestyle, or social and political structures.

RECENT EVENTS Sahelian *droughts* (periods of inadequate rainfall) have been increasingly frequent since the 1960s. They have forced many Tuareg to migrate northward to

Tuareg weaponry

Historical Tuareg weapons exhibit a blend of styles from African to Arabic and even European. The European influence is a possible result of the crusades of the eleventh to thirteenth centuries, or may derive from captured pirate weaponry that made its way south to the Sahara. The blades of this sword and dagger were forged from metal and the hilts covered in leather.

1 Dagger with sheathed tip, which would have been worn on the arm.
2 Sword with leather carrying sheath.

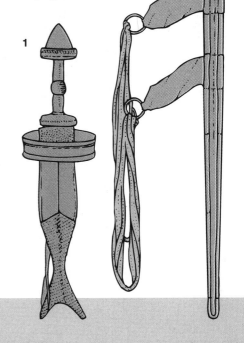

Camel caravan

A Tuareg camel *caravan* (company of travelers) crossing the vast expanse of the Sahara Desert.

© DIAGRAM

The tagelmust

This Tuareg man is wearing the *tagelmust,* a long cloth that is wrapped around to cover the head and sometimes the face. The tagelmust is of great importance to all Tuareg men; traditionally, it is rarely removed and should always be worn in the presence of non-Tuaregs. One of the names the Tuareg call themselves is "Kel Tagelmust," which means "People of the Tagelmust."

Tifnagh

The Tuareg script is called Tifnagh and is related to an ancient Libyan script. Inscriptions in Tifnagh have been found on rocks in the Sahara. These inscriptions often record early events in Tuareg history.

Algeria and Libya. Returning Tuareg refugees have come into conflict with the Malian and Niger governments in particular. A Tuareg uprising in Niger in 1992 sparked a conflict that lasted until a peace accord was signed in 1994. A similar Tuareg uprising in Mali has led to thousands of Tuareg refugees fleeing to neighboring countries. The conflict worsened before peace was reached in mid 1995.

Language

The Tuareg speak a Berber language called Tamacheq. It has four main dialects, which are largely mutually intelligible. The Tuareg often call themselves "Kel Tamacheq" – "People of the Tamacheq Language." Many Tuareg also speak Songhay, Hausa, or French. Tamacheq is written in a script called Tifnagh.

Ways of life

NOMADIC PASTORALISM Precolonial Tuareg were largely *nomadic pastoralists* (livestock herders who travel with their herds in search of pasture and water) who kept large herds of cattle, camels, sheep, and goats. The Tuareg would migrate with their herds of animals, moving from one water hole or pasture to another. *Oases* (fertile pockets in the desert) provided resting places and water. Surplus produce could be exchanged at oases for products such as dates and millet grown by the resident cultivators.

Many Tuareg are still nomadic, but colonial and government policies, drought, and pressure on the land from an increasing population have changed the way of life of many. Colonial governments limited each group of nomads to specific areas and the new national boundaries that were imposed further restricted nomadic activities. Since the colonial era, the improvement of existing wells and the provision of new ones has had side effects. Combined with improved veterinary care, permanent water holes have allowed herds to increase dramatically in size and overgrazing has seriously damaged pasturelands. Attempting to control the Tuareg, governments have often pursued policies that encourage them to settle and practice farming. Until recently, the Algerian government even had a policy of forced sedentarization, which grouped the Tuareg in agricultural cooperatives.

A severe drought struck the Sahelian lands in 1968–74 and again in 1984–5, permanently changing the Tuareg lifestyle. Thousands of people and whole herds of cattle died, while others were forced to sell their herds and thousands more moved south to Niger and Nigeria. Although many returned to nomadic pastoralism – with greatly depleted herds – others did not. As a result, many Tuareg are now settled farmers or seasonal laborers in the ports and docks of North and West Africa.

TRADE Most Tuareg engaged in trading across the Sahara as well as nomadic pastoralism in the precolonial era. Trade was deeply affected by the arrival of the French, however. Trans-Saharan trading was largely curtailed by the imposition of customs duties and competition from new coastal trading centers. Only the salt trade remained active. International trade has partly replaced the trans-Saharan trade but it is not as lucrative. Using their camels to travel cross-country in long caravans, the Tuareg take advantage of price differences between countries to make a profit. Potash, which is used in fertilizers and soaps, is taken from Bilma in eastern Niger to Katsina in northern Nigeria, for example.

CAMELS Although trucks now cross the Sahara, most Tuareg still rely on camels for transportation as they can go places where no wheeled vehicle can. The camel has large eyes, protected by long eyelashes and heavy eyebrows. Its long legs end in cushionlike feet that act on the loose sand like snowshoes on snow. Camels can travel for days with little food and for weeks

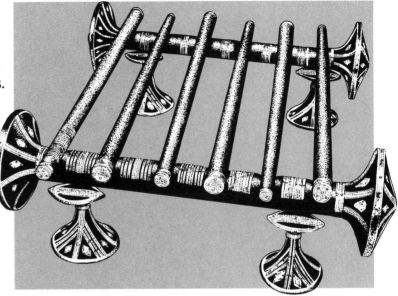

Tuareg bedstead
Made from wood and decorated with silver, copper, and bronze, this twentieth-century bedstead harks back to the design of Ancient Egyptian beds. Indeed, the ancestors of the Tuareg were already settled in North Africa when Ancient Egypt was flourishing thousands of years ago.

Meeting of elders
A meeting of Tuareg elders in an ancient graveyard in the Sahara. The Tuareg believe such graves to be those of legendary giants. This belief lends decisions made at these graveyards great significance.

Tent

This *nomadic* tent is made from cloth suspended on wooden poles. Many Tuareg now use plastic sheeting for their tents. A tent is usually made by elderly female relatives and owned by a married woman. Mud or stone permanent houses, however, are built and owned by men. As the nomadic Tuareg are increasingly being forced to settle down, the property balance between men and women is changing as tents – owned by women – are gradually being replaced by permanent houses, which are owned by men.

without water. A camel can eat almost any kind of plant, no matter how thorny. The camel's strength and endurance have earned it the name "ship of the desert."

The Tuareg take great care of their camels, making sure that they get enough rest and are unloaded when they stop. Typically, the animal's burden includes: trade goods, tents, blankets, provisions, and pots and pans.

Social structure

POLITICAL STRUCTURE In the past, the Tuareg were divided into seven main groupings or *confederations*: the Kel Ahaggar, Kel Ajjer, Kel Adrar, Kel Aïr, Kel Geres, Aullemmeden Kel Dennek, and the Aullemmeden Kel Ataram. The Kel Ahaggar and the Kel Ajjer of southern Algeria are known as the Northern Tuareg. The other groups, who live mostly in the Sahel, are known as the Southern Tuareg. Each confederation was led by an *amenokal* (king). These confederations have been disempowered since the colonial era; each amenokal now provides a link with the relevant central government.

SOCIAL STRUCTURE There are three main Tuareg social classes. At the top are the *imajeghen* (nobles) one of whom is elected as the amenokal of each confederation. The imajeghen were decimated by French reprisals after the rebellion of 1917 and today form less than one percent of the total Tuareg population. After the nobles come the *imghad* – the ordinary people. The third main

Tuareg drummer
Women are generally the musicians among the Tuareg. This Tuareg woman is using a hollowed-out gourd placed upside down in a wooden bowl as a drum.

group is the *iklan,* descendants of Black Africans who were once Tuareg slaves. Postcolonial governments have largely eradicated slavery, however, and many iklan are now farmers, herders, artisans, blacksmiths, or laborers.

Women and men have equal status and husbands and wives may both own property. Women join in the decision-making processes of the group and both men and women tend to be equally well educated. Usually, the men tend the animals, while the women look after the children, prepare food, and milk the animals.

Culture and religion

RELIGION The vast majority of Tuareg are Muslims – Islam was introduced to North Africa by Muslim Arabs in the seventh century. Most Tuareg groups have *ineslemen* or *marabouts* (a religious class that was introduced after the adoption of Islam). Ineslemen act as teachers, counselors, and mediators in local disputes.

DRESS The Tuareg are sometimes known as the "People of the Black Veil" because the men shield their faces with a *tagelmust* (a long strip of cloth). The tagelmust can be as much as 20 ft (6 m) long. The cloth is, in fact, not black but dark blue. In the past, the veil was made from strips of Sudanese *indigo* (deep blue) cotton, but today this material is expensive and cheaper imported fabrics are used instead. Sudanese cotton is still used for special garments though. Some of the blue dye of this fabric would come off on the faces of the wearers, giving the Tuareg their other nickname of "Blue Men." Women usually go unveiled but often wear a headcloth.

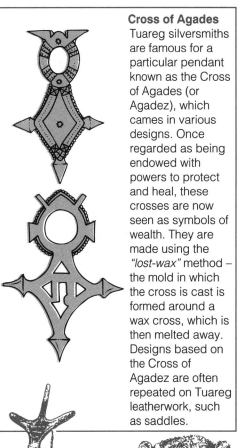

Cross of Agades
Tuareg silversmiths are famous for a particular pendant known as the Cross of Agades (or Agadez), which cames in various designs. Once regarded as being endowed with powers to protect and heal, these crosses are now seen as symbols of wealth. They are made using the *"lost-wax"* method – the mold in which the cross is cast is formed around a wax cross, which is then melted away. Designs based on the Cross of Agadez are often repeated on Tuareg leatherwork, such as saddles.

Tuareg saddle
The saddle on this camel is recognizably Tuareg as it has the uniquely Tuareg cross shape – the Cross of Agades (or Agadez) – rising from its pommel.

Traveling across the desert

For centuries, travelers have crisscrossed the Sahara — the world's largest desert — along well-tried routes, mostly in order to trade. Cities to the north and south of the Sahara serve as "ports" for this traffic. In the north, they include Marrakech and Fez in Morocco, Gabès in Tunisia, Ghudamis (Ghadames) in Libya, and Cairo in Egypt. To the south, the principal trading towns include Ségou in Mali, Kano in Nigeria, and the oasis city of Bilma in Niger. Many of the routes were in regular use at least 2,500 years ago. Although in decline today, many are still used. Mali's Tombouctou (Timbuktu) and Audaghost in Mauritania were once bustling trade depots but are now no longer major centers.

Routes

Desert travel is only possible with water, so the routes followed by the Saharan traders lead from one water source to another — oases (fertile pockets in the desert), wells, and watering holes. Many watering holes and wells have fallen into disuse since the advent of motorized travel.

Four of the north-south routes are particularly important. The easternmost route, the Selima trail, starts from Cairo, in Egypt. After following the Nile River, it heads southwest through the oases of Kharga in Egypt — the Great Oasis — and Selima and Bir Atrun in Sudan to Al Fashir. Next comes the Bilma trail, which runs from the Sokna oasis in Libya through Marzuq (Murzuk), to Bilma in Niger. Bilma is also an oasis, from which salt and dates are regularly exported. The Ghudamis trail starts at Gabès in Tunisia and leads through Ghudamis, a walled oasis and trading center in Libya, and Agadez (Agades) in northern Niger. It ends at Kano, regional

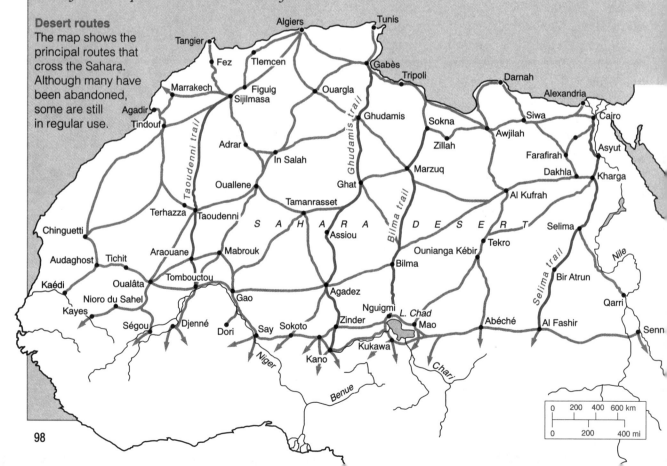

Desert routes
The map shows the principal routes that cross the Sahara. Although many have been abandoned, some are still in regular use.

capital of northern Nigeria. The westernmost route is the Taoudenni trail, which starts in southern Morocco and runs through Taoudenni in Mali to Tombouctou. Taoudenni lies in a large oasis and is a major producer of salt. There are many other routes, including a number of east-west trails, such as the route from Gao in Mali to Cairo in Egypt.

Goods

The earliest traders from the north ventured across the Sahara in search of two main things: gold and slaves. They obtained both from the Empire of Ghana, in present-day Mali and Mauritania, and later the Empire of Mali, in present-day Mali. They also bought ebony, ivory, and ostrich feathers. In

protect its eyes against wind-blown sand, and it can close its nostrils for the same purpose. Above all, a camel can eat plants that other animals would reject, such as dried grasses and the thorny plants and shrubs that are found in the desert and semidesert.

Camels used in Africa are mostly the one-humped breed, known as Arabian camels or dromedaries. Fat reserves stored in their humps enable camels to go for several days without eating or drinking. Not surprisingly, they work up a tremendous thirst and a large camel can down as much as 25 gallons (95 l) of water in ten minutes. A camel can carry a load up to 350 lb (160 kg) in weight — more on short journeys — slung in two packs on either side of its

"Ship of the desert"
A camel *caravan* (company of travelers) traveling across the Sahara Desert. Not for nothing is the camel known as the "ship of the desert." It is a seemingly tireless animal, able to carry heavy loads for hours at a time.

return, they traded grain, weapons, glass, cotton, and other manufactured goods. Many of the oases, such as Bilma, contributed to the trade with salt and dates. Today, most oases also grow grain and vegetables for export.

Transportation

Originally, traders probably made their way on foot, carrying goods on their backs. Later, they used donkeys, which are not really suitable for desert travel. Ever since camels were introduced into North Africa from southwest Asia nearly 2,000 years ago, thay have been the main form of transportation. The camel is well suited to desert travel. Long eyelashes

back. The camels and their drivers travel in large convoys known as caravans for protection against robbers. In the past, some caravans were huge; those engaged in the salt trade numbered many thousands of animals. As late as the early 1900s some of the salt caravans had 20,000 camels or more. Today, parts of the Saharan routes are paved, and much of the trade is carried out using trucks.

Desert trade, and therefore desert travel, has largely been curtailed since the colonial era. The imposition of customs duties and the development of new coastal trading centers has put many trans-Saharan traders out of business.

The threat of desertification

At its most literal, desertification *means the creation of a desert or desertlike conditions. In practice, it refers to both a process and a result. As a process, desertification occurs in stages that can range from a slight reduction or change in vegetation cover to its complete loss. The effect on soils can range from minor to severe erosion (actual loss of soil) and structural damage. As a result, desertification causes the productivity of land to suffer and the land may eventually become unusable for both crop farming and animal grazing.*

It is often assumed that desertification involves the outward expansion of existing deserts. This is misleading. While it does usually occur near the desert margin or fringe — as this is where the vulnerable drylands are found — desertification usually occurs in patches or "islands" far from the actual desert edge. These areas may expand until they finally join up with the true desert, giving the impression that the desert edge is advancing.

Overgrazing
Overgrazing around this borehole in Kordofan province, Sudan, has led to a loss of vegetation. Improvements in veterinary care have allowed people to amass large herds, which are often concentrated around boreholes.

Causes and effects

There is not one single cause of desertification, but a combination of many in which both human and climatic factors play a role.

OVERGRAZING *If too many animals are being grazed on pasture then the quantity and quality of vegetation suffers; soils are denuded; and the animals' hoofs compact the soil surface and damage its structure, making the soil vulnerable to erosion. Eventually the health of the animals declines and the pasture may become unusable.*

OVERCULTIVATION *Marginal lands previously used as occasional pastures by herders are increasingly being used for continuous farming. Unless given time to recover, fragile dryland soils become exhausted; crop yields fall; plant cover is lost; and the thin layer of fertile topsoil is easily eroded.*

Overcultivation and overgrazing are widespread in the Sahel (the semidesert region south of the Sahara Desert) and on the northern fringe of the Sahara in Morocco, Algeria, Tunisia, and Libya.

VEGETATION CLEARANCE *Land is often cleared of vegetation to prepare it for cultivation, to collect fuelwood, or to provide timber for export. This exposes the soil to erosion; lowers the underground water level; and indirectly lowers soil fertility as once the wood supply is exhausted, dried animal dung is burnt instead, which deprives the soil of fertilizers.*

SALINIZATION *Salinization (the buildup of salts in the soil) often occurs in poorly-drained, irrigated drylands. As the soil's water level rises, evaporation at the surface also increases, leaving behind the salts that were dissolved in the water. This increases the concentration of salts in the soil, which in turn impairs plant growth and causes the crop yield to drop. In extreme cases, soils can become completely waterlogged and a salt crust may form on the surface. In North Africa, salinization and waterlogging are prevalent in Egypt, Algeria, Tunisia, and Sudan.*

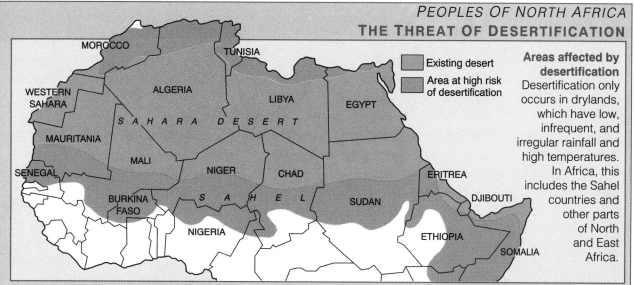

Existing desert

Area at high risk of desertification

Areas affected by desertification
Desertification only occurs in drylands, which have low, infrequent, and irregular rainfall and high temperatures. In Africa, this includes the Sahel countries and other parts of North and East Africa.

DROUGHT Inadequate rainfall or drought *causes plants to die and vegetation cover is reduced, so soils are more easily eroded. A lack of rainfall can turn appropriate land use into overuse, as the land can no longer support the same number of people or animals as previously. In recent decades, drought has persistently affected Sahelian countries.*

INDIRECT CAUSES *Increasing population levels, the resulting greater demand for food, and the spread of cash cropping have combined to force farmers to overcutlivate, overgraze, and clear more land. The growth of urban areas has increased the demand for fuelwood. Dense woods were once common around Khartoum, Sudan, but today few can be found within a 60-mile (100-km) radius of the city. It is now widely accepted that nomadic pastoralism (in which herders and their animals travel over a large area in search of water and pasture) is a sound strategy for dryland use. Colonial and government policies have forced many nomads to settle in one place, however, and this has often led to overgrazing and localized desertification. War, poverty, and civil strife have all further exacerbated the problem.*

Solutions
Desertification is certainly preventable and rarely irreversible. Tree planting to prevent soil erosion of deforested areas has been successful in the Algerian highlands. Simple solutions such as the use of cookers that consume less fuelwood can have a big impact on vegetation clearance. In order to combat desertification effectively, however, the indirect causes will ultimately have to addressed.

Green belt in the desert
Around this desert city, a grid of trees has been planted in the sand dunes in an attempt to anchor them and prevent spreading. Algeria and Sudan, in particular, have experimented with such methods. The planting of these "green belts" on the desert edge is little more than a token effort to deal with desertification, however, as spreading sand dunes are rarely a problem. The real areas of concern occur away from the desert edge.

Appendix: North African languages

Africans often identify themselves by the language they speak rather than, or in addition to, their ethnic origin or nationality. Language classification in Africa is complex – more than 1,000 languages are spoken, most of them "home" languages (native to the continent); the rest have been introduced by groups from Europe and Asia who settled in or colonized regions of Africa. Arabic, the language of the Arabs, is the most widely spoken language in North Africa. Many Muslims, as well as Arabs, learn Arabic as it is the language of the *Koran*, Islam's holy book. Arabic is also used widely as a common language.

Among the languages introduced to Africa are English, French, Spanish, Portuguese, Afrikaans, Urdu, Hindi, Gujarati, and Malagasy. English and French are commonly spoken in many North African countries as these were the languages of the main colonial powers. As a

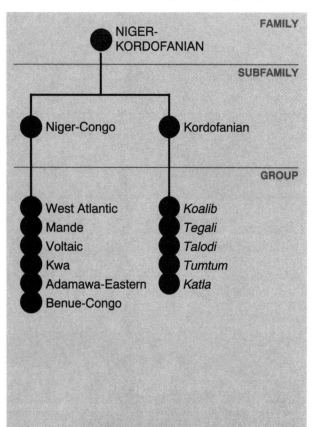

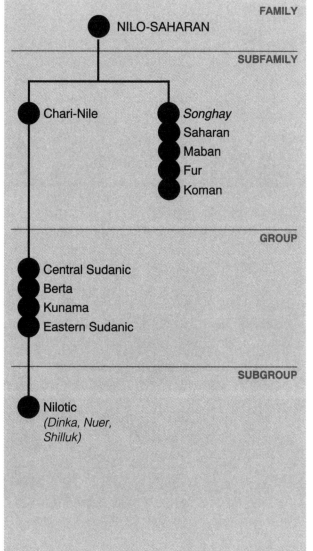

result of this diversity, many North Africans are multilingual (speak more than one language).

The home languages of Africa are divided into four language **families**: Niger-Kordofanian, Nilo-Saharan, Afroasiatic, and Khoisan. Within these families are several **subfamilies**, many of which are also divided into **groups** and again into **subgroups** – only the subgroups relevant to the languages covered in this volume have been included. Some language groups, such as Beja, are themselves languages; other groups or subgroups – Nilotic, for example – constitute clusters of individual languages.

Within the diagram below, the languages of the peoples profiled in this volume are printed in *italic* type. With this information, this appendix can be used to identify the subgroup or group, subfamily, and family of each language and to see how the different African languages relate to one another.

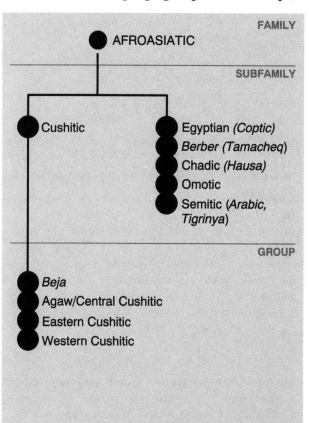

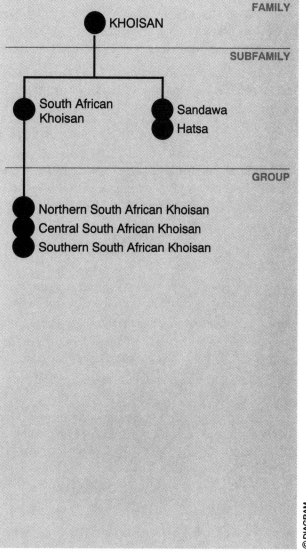

Glossary

Bold words are cross-references to other glossary entries.

Abuk An important **yath** in the Dinka religion. Abuk was the first woman and is associated with rivers.

akhnif A long, embroidered cape once worn by Jewish men in North Africa.

Allah The Muslim name for God.

amenokal In the past, the Tuareg were divided into seven main **confederations**. Each was led by an amenokal, or king.

Amon In Ancient Eygpt, Amon was a local Theban god depicted with a ram's head and symbolizing life and fertility. Over time, Amon became identified with **Re** and eventually became known as Amon-Re.

Amon-Re *see* **Amon**

ankh A T-shaped cross with a loop at the top. It is based on the Ancient Egyptian **hieroglyph** for eternal life.

Apedemak An ancient Nubian god.

arghul An ancient instrument from rural Egypt, a type of double clarinet.

Astarte The Phoenician Moon goddess, renamed "Tanit-Pene-Baal" (meaning "Tanit the Face of Baal") by the Carthaginians.

Baal-Haman *see* **Baal-Moloch**

Baal-Moloch The Phoenician Sun god, renamed Baal-Haman by the Carthaginians.

bandair A large Berber tambourine with an extra set of strings (snares) across its surface for added vibrations.

bany In the political structure of the Dinka, each group has a priestly or religious **clan**, called a bany, whose historical role was to control and safeguard the land.

beng The head of the **bany** in Dinka society. The name means "Master of the Fishing Spear."

bridewealth A practice common among African people in which a marriage between a couple is sealed with a gift – often cattle, but it may be cash or other animals – from the groom to the bride's family.

brimbiri A Nuba stringed musical instrument.

caliph The Arabic for "successor": an Islamic ruler.

caravan A company of travelers journeying together through the desert, often with a train of camels.

cataract An unnavigable or hazardous stretch of river, perhaps created by rapids, waterfalls, or a narrowing of the riverbanks. There are six major (numbered) cataracts on the Nile River between Aswan and Khartoum, some of which once formed political frontiers.

chaabi A form of popular music in Morocco; a mix of Arab, Berber, and contemporary Western styles, the lyrics tending to highlight political and social issues.

cheikhas Women musicians from rural Algeria from several centuries ago. The male equvalent is cheikhs.

chikha A female singer in Morocco. (Note that it can also have negative connotations; chikha can also mean "prostitute.")

chleuh Professional Berber musician-dancers of the High Atlas Mountains of Morocco.

cicatrix *see* **scarification**

clan A group of people, usually several **lineages**, related by ancestry or marriage. Clan members often often claim descent from a common ancestor or ancestors.

confederation An alliance of political groupings.

Coptic The word "Coptic" is derived from "aiguptios," the Greek word for Egyptian, which comes from an Ancient Egyptian name for Memphis. Today, the word "Coptic" has acquired many different meanings. As a noun, it is the name of an Afroasiatic language written in the Greek alphabet that is now largely extinct. Used as an adjective, Coptic can refer to the Copts (the Christian minority in Egypt); the Coptic (Christian) churches of Egypt and Ethiopia; to a historical period in Egypt's history; and to certain artifacts.

Not all Copts are members of the Egyptian Coptic Church, some are Roman Catholics or belong to various evangelical sects. Those that are members of the Coptic Church are sometimes called Orthodox Copts. The historical Coptic Period is basically Egypt's Christian era, which can be dated from either the 200s to 642 or from 451 to 642. "Coptic" is also used to refer to artifacts that were produced in Egypt during its Coptic Period, but not necessarily by Coptic artists. Finally, "Coptic" can be used to describe the Ethiopian Christian Church, which traces its history back to the Egyptian Coptic Church.

couscous A spicy dish from North Africa that consists of a steamed, coarse-ground grain such as semolina.

crux ansata A cross used from the fifth century onward in Egypt (during the **Coptic** Period), the shape of which is based on the Ancient Egyptian **hieroglyph** for "life" (the **ankh**). These crosses often decorated gravestones.

Dak The legendary son of **Nyikang**.

darabouka A Moroccan clay drum.

demotic A simplified system of Ancient Egyptian **hieroglyphic** writing.

Deng An important **yath** in the Dinka religion, Deng is associated with rain, thunder, and lightning.

derra A colored blouse once worn by Jewish women in North Africa.

dervishes Members of a branch of Islam called **Sufism**. Dervishes are dedicated to a life of poverty and chastity.

desertification A process of land degradation in which which previously fertile land can be turned into barren land or desert. It is usually caused by inadequate rainfall or the overuse of fragile drylands.

diel The founding family of a Shilluk village.

Dja-gay The first human according to the Nuer religion. Dja-gay is said to have emerged from a hole in the ground at a holy place called Duar.

drought Water shortage caused by a prolonged period of inadequate rainfall. Drought can have a devastating affect on the land and the people who make their living from the land, in particular, reducing the number of people following **nomadic** ways of life.

embalming The treatment of a dead body, usually after removing the internal organs, with various chemicals to prevent it from decaying. The Ancient Egyptians embalmed bodies so that the dead could use their own bodies in the afterlife. Early embalmers probably used tarlike substances as embalming solutions, but more successful techniques using dry natron (a naturally-occurring salt) were developed over time.

erg An area of shifting sand dunes in a desert.

erosion Can be used to refer to the loss of soil cover, which has been eroded by the action of wind or rain.

Ethiopian faunal realm A biogeographical zone that includes most of sub-Saharan Africa. Animals of this realm include lions, elephants, and giraffes.

feluccas Small, narrow boats propelled by oar or wind that have been used on the Nile River for centuries.

Garang An important **yath** in the Dinka religion. Garang was the first man and is associated with the Sun. Garang is also a common Dinka family name.

garigue Heath and poor **scrub** with patches of bare rock and soil.

ghaita A Berber reed instrument.

gorfa A Bedouin **granary**.

granary A building or room in which grain is stored.

guedra A Moroccan drum made from a cooking pot with a skin stretched over its opening.

gum arabic A gum exuded by certain acacia trees. It has many uses and is used in the manufacture of ink, food thickeners, and pills.

gumbri A small, three-stringed Berber lute.

Hadith A Muslim holy book providing guidance on all aspects of life, attributed to the Prophet Muhammad.

haikal A screen that seperates the sanctuary from the choir in a **Coptic** church.

Hajj One of the five holy duties of Muslims, the Hajj is a pilgrimage to Mecca, in Saudi Arabia – the Islamic holy city. After making the pilgrimage, a person can use a prefix such as Haji before their name.

hammada An area of rock platforms and boulders in a desert, covered with a thin layer of sand and pebbles.

haratin Lower-class Berber **oasis** cultivators.

henna A reddish-orange dye made from plants and used as a paint with which to decorate skin or dye hair.

hieratic A rapid, handwritten form of Ancient Egyptian **hieroglyphic** writing largely used by priests.

hieroglyph Picture symbol used in **hieroglyphic** writing.

hieroglyphics A form of writing, especially used in Ancient Egypt and Nubia, that uses pictures and symbols to represent concepts, objects, or sounds.

Horus An Ancient Egyptian Sun god, usually depicted with a falcon's head; the lord of heaven.

iklan The third and lowest class within the Tuareg social structure.

imajeghen The Tuareg nobility, one of whom is elected as the **amenokal** of each **confederation**.

imam A Muslim religious leader. An imam often leads the prayers at a **mosque**.

imdyazn A type of Berber band usually made up of four musicians, including a poet as leader.

imghad A Tuareg social classification refering to the ordinary citizen.

indigo A blue dye usually made from certain plants.

ineslemen *see* **marabout**

invertebrates Any animal without a backbone.

Isis An Ancient Egyptian fertility goddess, usually depicted as a woman with cow's horns; wife and sister of **Osiris** and mother of **Horus**.

izar Long, striped garment, usually red or white, once worn by Jewish women in North Africa.

jalabiya A long, loose robe often worn by Arab men.

Juok The god of the Shilluk people. Juok is an abstract divine being who is thought to have created the world.

Keskes A lidded pot in which **couscous** is steamed.

Khalifa A variation of **caliph**, the Arabic word for "successor." (In particular, it is used to refer to Abdullah ibn Muhammad who succeeded the **Mahdi** in 1885.)

khamsa Arabic for "five." A symbol of the hand that is used in jewelry worn by Berber women is also called khamsa. It represents the five holy duties of Muslims.

khamsin A strong local wind of Egypt.

kissar A Sudanese stringed instrument similar to a lyre.

Koran The sacred book of Islam.

Kowth The creator-god of the Nuer religion. The Nuer pray to Kowth for health and good fortune.

kuuarmuon A magistrate figure among the Nuer peoples; also known as the "leopard-skin chief" as, in the past, he would wear a leopard skin to indicate his status.

leaven Any substance, such as yeast, that helps dough to rise. Many people in North Africa make round, flat bread using a minimum of leaven.

lineage An extended family that shares a common ancestor. If this ancestor is male and descent is traced from father to son, then the lineage is patrilineal. If the ancestor is female and descent is traced from mother to daughter, then the lineage is matrilineal. Groups of several related lineages are often organized into **clans**.

lost-wax A method of metal casting in which an accurate model of the object to be cast is made of wax. The mold in which the metal will be cast is formed around the wax model. The wax is then metled away and molten metal poured into the empty mold. Lost-wax casting has been practiced in Africa for many centuries.

Macardit A **yath** in the Dinka religion. Macardit is the source of death and sterility.

Maghreb The Arabic name for the region comprising Morocco, Algeria, and Tunisia.

Mahdi In Islam, a Mahdi is a holy messiah (an expected savior or liberator). (In particular, it refers to Muhammad Ahmad who founded the nineteenth-century Mahdist State in present-day Sudan.)

maquis Shrubby mostly evergreen vegetation.

marabout A Muslim hermit or holy man. Among the Tuareg people, they act as teachers, counselors, and mediators in local disputes and are also called ineslemen.

mashta A female singer in Tunisia.

medina Literally meaning "town" in Arabic, a medina is usually the ancient quarter of a North African city.

mezonad A Tunisian musical instrument similar to a bagpipe.

mihrab A semicircular niche in one wall of a **mosque**; it indicates the direction of Islam's holy city, Mecca.

minaret A slender tower, topped by a platform and attached to a **mosque**.

minbar A flight of steps in a **mosque**, leading up to a seat from which the speaker can address the congregation.

mint tea A North African drink made with tea leaves and sprigs of fresh mint that is served hot and sweet.

monogamous The practice or state of having only one marriage partner.

Monophysite doctrine The **Coptic** Christian doctrine that asserts the unity of both the human and the divine in the nature of Christ.

monotheistic The practice or state of believing in only one god.

mosque A Muslim place of worship.

muezzin A crier who calls the Muslim faithful to prayer. The muezzin stands on the platform of a **minaret**.

mulid A huge **Sufi** festival.

mummy A dead body artificially preserved, as by the Ancient Eygptians. "Mummy" is a shortening of the term "mummification," which refers to the whole process of preserving and **embalming** a dead body.

naqqara A kettledrum played by Berber musicians.

nazir Leader of a Baggara group. The nazir acts as the official link with the Sudanese government.

Nhialac A Dinka divinity or **yath**, Nhialac can be several things: the sky; what is in the sky; an entity sometimes called "father" or "creator"; and also a power that can be possessed by any yath or even a particular man.

nomad Used to describe many, usually desert-living, peoples who follow a particular lifestyle. Nomads are "wanderers" (the word derives from "nomas," Latin for "wandering shepherd"), but they usually travel well-used paths, and their movements are dictated by the demands of trade or the needs of their herds for pasture and water.

nomadic Characteristic of, or like, **nomads** and their way of life.

nomadism Used to describe the lifestyle of a **nomad**.

nuba A form of traditional Arab music comprising a suite of several movements.

Nyikang The hero-god of the Shilluk religion. He is thought to have founded the Shilluk and to be reincarnated in the figure of the **reth**.

oasis A fertile pocket in the desert where the underground water reaches the surface.

ocher A yellow or reddish-brown clay. Many people use ocher to color and style their hair.

omda An official of a Baggara group responsible for collecting taxes and settling disputes.

Osiris An Ancient Egyptian god, ruler of the underworld and judge of the dead.

oud A stringed instrument of southwest Asia and North Africa that resembles a lute.

Palearctic faunal realm A biogeographical zone that includes Africa north of the Sahara, Europe, and most of Asia north of the Himalayas.

papyrus A tall, reedlike water plant, or the writing material made from it by the Ancient Egyptians. The Ancient Egyptians also used papyrus to make boats.

pastoral Characterisitc of, or like, **pastoralists** and their way of life.

pastoralism Used to describe the lifestyle of a **pastoralist**.

pastoralist A person who raises livestock.

pharaoh The title of the kings of Ancient Egypt.

polygyny The practice of having more than one wife.

Ptah An Ancient Egyptian god, worshipped as the creator of both gods and mortals.

pylon A monumental gateway, such as one at the entrance to an Ancient Egyptian temple. Ancient Egyptian pylons often resembled shortened pyramids.

qadi A Muslim judge.

qumqum An Arabic perfume sprinkler.

rabab A bowed instrument, similar to a fiddle, largely used in the **Maghreb**.

rabbi An ordained Jew, usually the spiritual head of a congregation, qualified to decide questions of law and ritual and to perform ceremonies such as marriages.

rai A hugely popular form of music in Algeria and Morocco, rai has its roots in the Algerian rural musicians of several centuries ago, but has been adopted by a new generation of young, disaffected Algerians as a form of protest music. It is becoming very popular in France, where many people from North Africa live.

Ramadan The ninth month of the Muslim year, during which Muslims fast between sunrise and sunset. Ramadan is the month that **Allah** called Muhammad to be His Prophet.

Re The Ancient Egyptian Sun god, depicted as a man with a falcon's head. Also known as Ra.

rebec A medieval fiddle and ancestor of the **rabab**.

reg An area of gravel and pebbles in a desert.

reth A king who is the ruler of the Shilluk people of

southern Sudan, believed by his subjects to be the incarnation of the legendary hero-god **Nyikang**.

rwais A group of professional Berber musicians who mix poetry, dance, and music in their performances.

salinization The buildup of salts in the soil that often occurs in poorly-drained, irrigated drylands. As the water level rises, evaporation also increases, leaving behind the salts from the water. The concentration of salts in the soil impairs plant growth and causes crop yields to drop.

savanna Open grasslands, often with scattered bushes or trees, characteristic of tropical Africa.

scarification The practice of making scratches or shallow cuts to adorn the body or face. The scar formed when such a cut heals is called a cicatrix.

scribe A professional writer who copied manuscripts before the advent of printing.

scrub Dense vegetation consisting of stunted trees, bushes, and other plants.

seminomadic pastoralism A form of **pastoralism** involving the seasonal movement of livestock.

Sharia The body of doctrines and laws that regulate the lives of those who profess Islam – Islamic holy law.

shawm A musical instrument used in the **Maghreb**; an ancestor of the modern oboe.

simoom A hot, violent, sandladen wind of the desert.

sirocco A hot, steady, oppressive wind that blows from the Libyan Desert (which is part of the Sahara Desert) across the Mediterranean into southern Europe, often accompanied by rain and dust.

souk The Arabic word for marketplace. Souks are usually in the old part of a town or village and are often in the open air.

steppe An extensive grassy plain, usually without trees.

Sufi A Muslim ascetic (one who leads a life of strict self-discipline) who adheres to **Sufism**.

Sufism A branch of Islam that is a special form of Islamic mysticism.

Sunna A code of behavior based on the Prophet Muhammad's words and deeds.

Sunni One of the two main branches of Islam (the other being Shiite), which consists of those who accept the authority of the **Sunna**. Sunnis make up about ninety percent of all Muslims.

synagogue A Jewish house of worship.

taboo A social prohibition or restriction laid down by culture, tradition, or convention that forbids, for example, certain actions and helps to define acceptable behavior.

tagelmust A long strip of cloth worn over the head and face by Tuareg men.

tambour A Nubian stringed musical instrument.

Tanit-Pene-Baal *see* **Astarte**

tbeck A large basket in which couscous grains, sorted according to size, are stored.

Torah From the Hebrew "to instruct," Torah refers to the first five books of the Old Testament regarded collectively. It can also refer to the scroll on which this is written, as used in **synagogue** services, or the whole body of traditional Jewish teaching, including Oral Law.

tsetse fly A Bantu word, "tsetse" literally means "the fly that kills." Tsetse flies carry organisms that can cause severe illnesses in both animals and humans. They flourish near rivers and in swamps and their presence can make a region uninhabitable.

tukl A Nuba building with a thatched, cone-shaped roof.

wadi A normally dry **watercourse** in the desert that is subject to flash flooding after heavy rain.

watercourse A dry or seasonally dry river.

wattle-and-daub A building technique using a woven latticework of sticks thickly plastered with clay.

yad A hand indicator for use while reciting the **Torah**.

yath A divinity or power of the Dinka religion. The plural is yeeth.

yeeth *see* **yath**

zakah A form of religious tax in Islam. Paying zakah is one of the five holy duties of Muslims and is derived from the Arabic word meaning "to purify."

Index

Peoples pages and special features are printed in **bold**; *italic* page numbers refer to illustrations, captions, or maps.

Index